The Big Book of Tell Me Why Again

Selected from
The Big Book of Tell Me Why #2

Arkady Leokum

BARNES
&NOBLE
B O O K S
NEW YORK

CONTENTS

Chapter 3

The Human Body

Chapter 4

How Other Creatures Live

Chapter 5

How Things Are Made

CHAPTER 1
OUR WORLD

WHAT IS RADIATION?

Looking at it very simply, radiation is the sending out of waves of energy. You have known about it since you were a baby—though you didn't know what it was. When you held your hand in front of a hot stove or radiator, or a light bulb, you felt radiant heat. When you sat in the warm sun, a type of radiation called ultraviolet rays was striking your skin.

All these are examples of electromagnetic radiation. The other major type of radiation is called radioactive radiation, and it comes from either radioactive material or nuclear reactions. In radioactive radiation, particles, as well as waves of energy, are given off.

Since electromagnetic radiation is the sending out of waves of energy, we should know something about those waves. The distance between the waves is called the wavelength. The number of waves passing a given point each second is the frequency. And when all the waves within a certain range of wavelengths are grouped together, we call them the spectrum.

The group with the shortest wavelength is the X-ray spectrum. Next comes the ultraviolet spectrum. Then comes the visible-light spectrum; we can see these waves. The waves get still longer, and we can no longer see them. This is the infrared spectrum. Even longer waves (Hertzian waves) are used for radio, television, and radar.

What produces all these waves? In some cases machines are required; in others they are produced naturally. Naturally made waves come from the sun. To produce any radiation requires energy. In the case of the sun, atomic energy is produced by a reaction called fusion. In the case of X-rays, a target must be bombarded with particles.

Radioactive radiation is the process of change or decay that certain elements undergo. Such elements are radioactive. They radiate particles (and waves, too) as the nuclei of their atoms break up.

WHAT ARE UFO'S?

The popular name for them is "flying saucers." UFO stands for "unidentified flying object."

Do they really exist? Many books have been written about them and thousands of people claim they have seen them; some even claim they have photographed them. And no matter what scientific investigations reveal, there will still be people who believe they exist.

Studies of saucer reports show that UFO's are very different from one another. Some people report having seen flat saucers; others see saucers shaped like spheres, cigars, or doughnuts.

The colors of saucers seem to be as different as their sizes. Saucers of nearly all colors have been reported. Some seem to change color as they are being watched.

Saucers have been seen to move in every direction and at nearly every speed. They can turn at right angles, move straight up or straight down, or travel in a zigzag path. They can hang motionless in the air, and make either a hissing noise or a roar.

When the United States Air Force started to investigate the reports about flying saucers, it discovered that people weren't "imagining" what they saw. Everyone who reported a flying saucer had seen something. But what?

In some cases, the "something" was actually a weather balloon. In other cases, it was a satellite, a cloud, a meteor, a star, a bird, a comet, a planet, or fireworks. It was also what are called sun dogs. These are images of the sun reflected through ice crystals. Many flying-saucer stories have been traced to fireballs, which are formed by lightning.

If saucers were really spaceships, there would be a certain pattern in the reports about them. But there is no such pattern. The reason is that people are not seeing spaceships but many other things. So scientists believe that there is no evidence that we are being visited, watched, or invaded by intelligent beings from other worlds.

WHY DO ALL THE PLANETS LOOK DIFFERENT?

The reason each of the planets looks different to us is that each one seems to be made up of different substances. Even though they are all planets revolving around the sun and part of the solar system, their composition varies.

We actually know very little about what the planets are made of, and this is one of the questions man hopes to answer with the space explorations that are presently going on and those that are being planned for the future.

Let's take a brief look at each of the other planets and see what is known of their make-up. Mercury is a small, rocky world. It has some dark areas on its surface, and has a very thin atmosphere of carbon dioxide.

Venus is a white globe with some hazy markings. It is completely covered by a layer of white clouds. The clouds contain carbon-dioxide gas, and some nitrogen and oxygen may also be present. We still don't know whether the surface of Venus is very hot or not. If it is not hot, there may be oceans on Venus. If it is very hot, then it is probably a vast and lifeless desert.

Mars is a small, rocky world. Parts of Mars are darker than others, but we still don't know whether these markings are canals or not. Mars has little if any oxygen, so the question about life on Mars is still a mystery.

Jupiter appears as a yellowish globe with darker bands of color crossing it. Jupiter is covered by a layer of clouds that may be thousands of miles deep. We still don't know whether Jupiter has a rocky core or whether the main body of the planet is made up of solid hydrogen.

Saturn is also covered by clouds. It has bands of color—yellowish at the equator, greenish at the poles. It may have a small, rocky core. Uranus looks slightly green with a band of silvery color. Neptune is a dim greenish object, with a few bands of color. Very little is known about Pluto. It may be a small, rocky planet like the earth. It is so cold that any atmosphere it has must be frozen.

As you can see, man still has a great deal to find out about the other members of the solar system.

WHAT ARE THE SIZES OF THE PLANETS?

A planet is very different from a star. A star is a huge ball of hot gases that gives off heat and light. A planet is a much smaller body that shines by reflected light.

Let's start with the planet nearest to the sun and move outward. The first one is Mercury. Mercury's diameter is 2,900 miles—about the width of the Atlantic Ocean. So it's only a fraction of the earth's size.

The next planet we meet is Venus. It is very nearly the same size as the earth. Its diameter is 7,600 miles, while that of the earth is 7,913 miles. By the way, an odd fact about Venus is that it rotates backward; that is, from east to west. The next planet is our earth, and then comes Mars.

Mars shines in the sky with a reddish color. It has a diameter of 4,200 miles, a little more than half that of the earth. Mars has interested scientists more than most planets because of its markings that look like channels or canals. It seems the most likely planet other than ours to have life on it, perhaps some kind of plant life.

Jupiter, the next planet, is far away from the sun. It takes about 11.9 years to complete one orbit. Jupiter is the largest of the planets. It has a diameter of 86,800 miles, nearly 11 times the diameter of the earth.

Saturn, the next planet, is another giant. It has a diameter of 71,500 miles, which is about nine times that of the earth. An unusual thing about Saturn is the group of flat rings that circle it. These rings are made up of billions of tiny particles.

Uranus, the next planet, is much larger than the earth. It has a diameter of 29,400 miles. Uranus is tilted over on its side. Its axis is tilted over at an angle of 98 degrees. (The earth tilts at an angle of

23½ degrees.) Neptune, the next planet, is 28,000 miles in diameter. And finally, the last known planet, Pluto, is believed to have a diameter of about 3,600 miles. It is so far from the sun that the sun appears to it as only a bright star in the sky.

WHAT IS THE CORONA OF THE SUN?

Have you ever seen photographs of a total eclipse of the sun? All around the dark sun, there is an uneven glow of light, and this light is called the corona.

To understand what the corona is, we have to know some things about the sun. To begin with, the sun, at least at its surface, is not a solid like the earth. This surface, which is all that we can observe of the sun, is composed of gases.

In fact, the sun is surrounded by four layers of gaseous matter that hide what is underneath. The innermost of these layers is called the photosphere. The next two layers are known as the reversing layer and the chromosphere. Together they form the sun's atmosphere. The outermost layer is the corona.

Let's see what each of these layers of gas is. The photosphere (or "light sphere") is what we see when we look toward the sun. Most of the time, dark sunspots can be seen on this bright surface.

The "reversing layer," which is made of gaseous vapors, extends

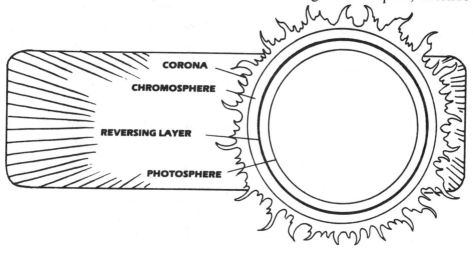

CORONA
CHROMOSPHERE
REVERSING LAYER
PHOTOSPHERE

several hundred miles out from the photosphere of the sun. This layer is never seen, but it can be studied by an instrument called the spectrograph.

Outside the reversing layer is the chromosphere, or color sphere. It is about nine thousand miles thick and is made up mostly of hydrogen and helium gases. At the time of a total eclipse, it shines out around the dark disk with a brilliant scarlet light. From this red border, flame-colored clouds of the same material shoot out to great heights, sometimes even as much as one million miles! They are called prominences, and they look like great flames of fire.

Then comes the outer layer, which is called the corona. It is composed of light, gaseous matter, and has two parts. The inner corona, lying next to the red chromosphere, is a band of pale yellow. The outer corona is white, with streamers extending out millions of miles from the edge of the sun.

All of this describes only the layers that surround the sun. What is beneath them still remains a mystery!

WHAT ARE ULTRAVIOLET RAYS?

Light rays, heat rays, X-rays, and ultraviolet rays are all forms of radiation. Radiation wavelengths have an amazingly large span. The longest are radio waves; the shortest, gamma rays. About halfway between the longest and shortest wavelengths are light waves, or visible radiation.

Light waves themselves have a great variety of wavelengths. Each color is a different wavelength. Red light is the longest wavelength visible to man. Next is orange, followed by yellow, green, blue, and violet, which is the shortest wavelength radiation that can be seen.

Just past the violet-light wavelength are the radiations in what scientists call the ultraviolet range. The sun emits these rays, as do certain man-made lamps specially produced for this purpose. Ultraviolet wavelengths range from just above those of violet light to more than 2,500,000 waves per inch.

Because ultraviolet rays are shorter than other rays, they are penetrating. From the sun these rays, along with heat, reach the nerves in your skin. Still, only about half the ultraviolet rays from the sun ever reach the ground. Many are absorbed high up in the earth's atmosphere.

IS THE EARTH ALWAYS THE SAME DISTANCE FROM THE SUN?

Do you know why it's hot in summer and cold in winter? It's because the position of the earth's axis with respect to the sun changes as the earth revolves around the sun. Now, this change is very slight, when you consider the great distance of the earth from the sun. Yet that small change is enough to make us broil in summer and freeze in winter!

Can you imagine then what life would be like if the distance of the earth from the sun were to change a great deal? If we wandered farther away, life might become impossible because of the cold. If we came much nearer, we might all burn up in the heat! So the distance from the earth to the sun remains pretty much the same at all times, and that distance is, in round numbers, ninety-three million miles.

But the orbits of the planets around the sun are not quite circular, and in the case of many other planets the distance from the sun does change quite a bit during the year.

For example, the planet Mercury, nearest the sun, has an orbit that is less like a circle than the path of any other planet. The planet Venus varies in its distance from the sun from sixty-seven million to sixty-eight million miles.

Mars, the first planet beyond the earth, takes 687 days for its journey around the sun. During this trip its distance from the sun varies, but it averages about 141,700,000 miles.

Jupiter, the next planet away from the sun, provides an example of a planet whose distance from the sun varies a great deal. So we find that in discussing distance from the sun, an "average" figure is given for all the planets, including the earth. The reason for the variations is the pull on each planet by the others in our solar system.

WHY DON'T WE FEEL THE ROTATION OF THE EARTH?

Until a few hundred years ago, men believed that the earth stood still; that the sun, the moon, and the stars went around it. It's easy to understand why this was so. After all, that's the way it looked. And nobody could feel the earth moving. If the earth moved, why didn't objects fly off it, including the water in the oceans?

Today, of course, we know that the earth is moving constantly in two ways. It is going around the sun, and it is rotating on its axis. The reason we don't feel it is that we go along with the surface as it moves, and so does the air that surrounds us. Gravity holds everything on earth down, including the water in the oceans.

But the rotation of the earth is known to us from many things that we observe and feel. It is this rotation that causes day and night. If the earth didn't rotate, the side facing the sun would always have daylight, and the side facing away from the sun would be in darkness. But every point on the earth is carried around to the light side and then the dark side every twenty-four hours.

Another important motion of the earth that we can't "feel," but that makes a difference in our lives, is the trip the earth takes around the sun. It is this motion that causes the change of seasons, and you know how different our life becomes with each changing season. In fact, this trip around the sun, which takes about 365¼ days, and which we call a year, is the way we measure history, the length of our lives, and so on.

The change of seasons is caused by the slant of the earth's axis. This slant or tilt is 23½ degrees from the vertical. Each pole leans toward the sun half the year and away from the sun the other half. So for six months the northern part of the earth receives more sunlight and thus more heat (summer), and during the other months it receives less sunlight and has its cooler season.

HOW MUCH DOES THE EARTH WEIGH?

Since the earth is suspended in space, "weighing" it is not the same thing as putting an object on a scale. When we speak of the weight of the earth, we mean the amount of matter that makes it up. This is called its mass.

The earth's mass is about 6.6 sextillion tons. To give you an idea of how that number looks, here it is: 6,600,000,000,000,000,000,000. How did scientists find out that this was the mass of the earth?

To do this, they used a principle based on the fact that any two objects attract each other. This is what the force of gravity depends on. Put in simple terms, the law of gravity states that two objects are attracted by a force that depends on their mass and their distance apart. The bigger the objects, the greater the force that pulls them together. The farther apart they are, the smaller the force.

To measure the weight of the earth, the following is done: A small weight is suspended from a string. The exact position of that weight is measured. Now a ton of lead is brought near the hanging weight. There is an attraction between the weight and the lead, and this causes the weight to be pulled just a tiny bit out of line. (Actually, it is less than one-millionth of an inch, so you can see how carefully the measuring must be done.)

After this is measured, scientists can use mathematics to figure out the weight of the earth. They have measured the power of the earth's attraction on the weight, and they have measured the power of the one-ton lead's attraction on the suspended weight. The relative difference can be calculated and tells them the mass of the earth.

What is this mass made of? There is the crust of solid rock; then a layer called the mantle, which is also solid rock and goes down about one thousand eight hundred miles; and then the innermost part, which is the core and is about two thousand one hundred miles in radius. The material of the core is liquid because of the great heat at the center of the earth.

WHAT IS ST. ELMO'S FIRE?

St. Elmo's fire is one of the many interesting phenomena connected with lightning, and to understand it we must review what takes place when lightning occurs.

All matter is made up of two kinds of particles, positive and negative. The two kinds of particles strongly attract each other, and if they are separated, they have a great tendency to reunite.

14

When a strong negative or positive charge is built up in the base of a cloud, it induces an opposite charge below it on the earth. Electrons start moving from the region of the negative charge to the positive. They gradually build up a channel or channels of charged particles between the earth and the cloud, and when there is a great surge of electrons, a lightning flash occurs.

Now suppose that instead of allowing the charges to build up until the strain is too great and must be broken, there were some way of enabling the charge from the earth below to "leak off." Instead of a lightning stroke, the charge would leak off in the form of a "brush discharge." This, by the way, is exactly the way a lightning rod works. The point of the lightning rod enables the electrons to leak off.

St. Elmo's fire is the glow that accompanies such a "brush discharge" of atmospheric electricity. It appears as a tip of light on the ends of pointed objects, such as church towers or the masts of ships during stormy weather. We usually hear a crackling or fizzing noise at the same time.

Another place St. Elmo's fire is commonly observed is on the edge of propellers, and along the wing tips, windshields, and noses of airplanes when they are flying in dry snow or in the vicinity of thunderstorms. This discharge may sometimes be strong enough to cause static in the radio of the airplane.

IS THE EQUATOR THE HOTTEST PLACE ON EARTH?

When we talk about places on earth being "hot" or "cold," we are talking about "climate." And in a general way all climate is determined by the heat of the sun.

It is the heat of the sun that warms the land, the oceans, and the atmosphere. The heat of the sun draws moisture into the atmosphere, and thus makes rain possible. The sun's heat causes differences in air pressure, which creates winds, and together the sun's heat and the winds produce ocean currents. So, in discussing the climate of a particular location, it is important to consider the sun's heating effect on that area.

Now, because the surface of the earth is curved, the heating effect of the sun is greatest at the Equator and least at the Poles. At the Equator, the rays from the sun strike the earth vertically. Above and below the equatorial region, the rays strike the earth at an angle, or slant. This means that the regions above and below the Equator, the Temperate Zones, receive fewer rays from the sun than the areas in the region of the Equator, the Tropical Zone. The regions of the earth farthest from the Equator, in other words, receive the least amount of heat.

When a ray of sunlight strikes the earth at an angle, it has to pass through more atmosphere, and so some of its heat is absorbed by the air—and that's another reason the other zones receive less heat.

All of this makes the region of the Equator the hottest region on earth. But we have been talking about what is called solar climate, climate depending only on the sun's heat. There are many other factors, however, that enter into the picture to determine what is called physical climate, the actual climates found on the earth.

The most important of these other factors are water, land, and altitude. The waters of the oceans and ocean currents, the existence of large land areas, and the altitude of the land all can combine to create different climates regardless of the location on earth. That's why, at any particular time, it may be hotter at a point far from the Equator than it is at the Equator itself, although the equatorial region is the hottest on earth.

WAS THE SAHARA ALWAYS A DESERT?

The Sahara desert is the world's hottest region in summer and the world's largest desert. It is bigger than the United States and has an area of over 3,500,000 square miles.

Yet at one time most of the Sahara was under water! In ages gone by, there were rivers and valleys and gorges. In fact, some people believe that the sand of the Sahara comes from the time when it was the bottom of a great sea. But this theory is not accepted by most authorities.

We do know that at one time the Sahara had the climate of a moist temperate or subtropical region. There were probably grass and trees growing there. But gradually the vegetation disappeared and the region became arid. This dried out the soil, and wind erosion broke up the particles until the sand was formed. There are still some patches of oases, however, where trees and grasses grow, and where springs and natural wells may be found.

The Sahara is kept dry by the winds in the region. They are northeast trade winds that blow steadily toward the Equator. As the air moves toward the Equator, it gets hotter and is able to hold more moisture. So the air takes up moisture like blotting paper and keeps the desert dry and hot.

In July, there are many places in the Sahara where the average temperature is 100 degrees Fahrenheit. At a place called Azizia near Tripoli, the world's record heat was recorded in 1922. It was 136.4 degrees! When the sun goes down, however, the land cools very quickly. The temperature may drop 30 to 50 degrees, and in some oases in winter, there is even frost at night!

Despite the dryness of the land, there is some animal life there, such as the desert antelope, which carries a water supply in a special sac in its body.

HOW ARE LAKES FORMED?

Lakes are inland bodies of water that occupy depressions in the surface of the land. These depressions are called basins.

Lakes result from the flow of water into low areas. Lake water comes largely from rainfall and melting snow. The water enters a lake basin through brooks, streams, rivers, underground springs, and ground water.

The lake basins themselves are formed in several ways. Many lakes are the result of faulting or warping in the earth's crust. Lake Superior in North America is an example of such a lake.

Sometimes lakes are created by volcanoes. A lava flow may block the outlet of a valley and form a lake basin. Sometimes the crater of an extinct volcano fills with water. Crater Lake in southern Oregon is an example of this.

Many lakes occupy basins formed by glacial erosion. All the Great Lakes (except Lake Superior) and Lake Winnipeg in Canada are examples of lakes that were formed by glaciers.

Along coastal areas, waves and shore currents sometimes close inlets and temporarily create lakes out of bays and estuaries. Sometimes the main stream of a river may build up its flood plain by depositing silt (mud and soil) when the river overflows. As a result, tributary valleys are flooded and lakes are formed.

In places where limestone underlies the land, ground water may dissolve and remove enough limestone to produce great sinkholes that form lake basins. Florida contains many lakes of this type.

Lakes may also be artificially made. When a dam is built across a river valley, it will block the flow of water and form a lake. Lake Mead was formed when Hoover Dam was built on the Colorado River.

WHAT ARE THE LARGEST WATERFALLS IN THE WORLD?

A waterfall is any stream of water which descends suddenly from a higher to a lower level. If the volume of water is small, it is called a cascade; if large, it is called a cataract.

Some falls plunge hundreds of feet in a single narrow stream of water. Others are famous for their breadth and for the immense volume of water that pours over their ledges. Here are some of the great waterfalls of the world:

Angel Falls, in the Guiana Highlands of Venezuela, are the world's highest falls (3,212 feet), with the longest uninterrupted drop

(2,648 feet). The falls were discovered in 1935 by an American aviator, James Angel.

The longest waterfall in Asia is the Gersoppa Falls in India. It is a cataract that falls in four sections for a total of 830 feet. The falls that discharge the largest volume of water of any waterfall are the Guaira Falls, which are on the border of Brazil and Paraguay. They discharge over 470,000 cubic feet of water per second. There are 18 falls, but the total drop is only about 200 feet.

One of the world's highest single waterfalls is Ribbon Falls in Yosemite National Park. It is a narrow stream that drops 1,612 feet down a cliff into the Merced River.

The second highest falls in the world are found in South Africa. They are the Tugela Falls. The falls plunge 2,800 feet in five jumps.

And then, of course, there are Niagara Falls, among the most famous in the world. They are located in the Niagara River, about 16 miles northwest of Buffalo, New York. Actually, Niagara Falls consist of two cataracts—the Horseshoe (or Canadian) Falls and the American Falls. The international boundary line between Canada and the United States passes through the center of Horseshoe Falls.

About 94 percent of Niagara's waters, or some 84,000,000 gallons, flows over the Horseshoe Falls every minute.

American Side of Niagara Falls

WHAT IS HARD WATER?

Water is a tasteless, odorless, colorless compound of two gases: hydrogen, a very light gas, and oxygen, a heavier, active gas. Water exists in three states: as a liquid; as a solid, called ice; and as a gas, called water vapor.

But when we discuss the various properties of water, we discover that water as it occurs in nature is never pure in the true sense. It contains dissolved mineral material, dissolved gases, and living organisms. So it is very seldom that we are dealing with just "water."

For example, chemically pure water is tasteless. But we all know there often is a slight taste to water. Part of this taste comes from the presence of certain impurities in the water. Raindrops falling through the atmosphere absorb some of the gases through which they pass.

Most important of these gases is oxygen, which makes it possible for living things to exist under water. Carbon dioxide is another important gas in water. Its presence in a water solution (carbonic acid) makes water capable of eroding limestone rocks and forming caves and sinkholes.

The action of this carbonic acid in water dissolves lime and magnesium carbonates, and this is what makes water "hard." Hard water does not produce a soap lather easily. If boiled, it leaves a lime coating on the inside of kettles.

Besides gases, natural waters contain dissolved salts. And river and lake water is also likely to contain inorganic particles that simply float in the water.

Water is distributed over the earth in a great "energy cycle." The sun draws up water into the air by evaporation from the seas and oceans. In the air, water vapor gathers into clouds and falls as rain, hail, snow, or dew, and works its way back to the sea.

WHERE DOES IT RAIN THE MOST?

Many things determine how much rain or snow any area of the world receives. These include temperature, height above sea level, location of mountain ranges, and so on.

Probably the rainiest place in the world is Mount Waialeale, Hawaii, on the island of Kauai. It has an average yearly rainfall of 471.68 inches. Cherrapunji, India, might be the next rainiest place, with its yearly average of 425 to 450 inches. At one time 150 inches of rain fell on Cherrapunji in a period of 5 days. And in one year, 1861, its rainfall added up to 905 inches.

To give you an idea of how much rain this is, let's note the rainfall in a number of cities around the world. New York City gets about 40 inches a year; San Francisco, about 20 inches; Boston, 42 inches; Chicago gets 30 inches; Ottawa in Canada gets 34 inches; Madrid, about 17 inches; and Paris, 22 inches. So you see what a contrast 450 inches in Cherrapunji is.

The driest place in the world is probably Arica, Chile. It averages only 0.02 inches of rain a year! The driest area in the United States is Greenland Ranch, Death Valley. There the average yearly rainfall is less than 1.5 inches.

Some large regions of the earth have heavy rainfall throughout the year. For example, almost every point along the Equator receives 60 inches or more of rain every year. The Equator is the meeting point of two large streams of air. All along the Equator, air moving down from the north meets air moving up from the south. There is a general upward movement of hot air laden with water vapor. As the air rises to colder heights, large amounts of water vapor condense and fall as rain.

A great deal of rain falls on the windward side of mountain ranges. The other side, called the lee, receives much less rain. An example is the Cascade Range of California. Westerly winds laden with water vapor sweep in from the Pacific Ocean. After striking the coast, the air rides up the western slopes of the mountains, cooling as it climbs higher. The cooling causes the water vapor to condense and fall as rain or snow.

WHAT IS A QUARRY?

Quarrying is the process by which rock materials are removed from the ground. The rocks may be quarried as solid blocks or slabs, or as crushed and broken stone. The block or slab rock is usually used for building. Crushed rock is most often used for roadbeds.

There are different types of quarries. In some, the rock is in a huge, solid mass. In others, the rock forms layers of different thicknesses. A pit quarry is actually a big hole in the ground. Sometimes it's wide and shallow, and sometimes it's a deep, narrow hole. Workers in pit quarries have to use ladders or stairs, or they may have to be lowered into the quarry by mechanical devices.

In pit quarries, there is often a water problem. This is because the quarry is like a big stone bowl, collecting and holding all the rainwater that pours into it. When this happens, the water has to be pumped out.

Sometimes rock suitable for quarrying is found above the ground. This is called a shelf quarry. In such a quarry, machines can be moved right up to the face of the quarry, and the rock can be hauled away directly.

How is it decided where to establish a quarry? Tests must be made first. Geologists can tell where the chances of finding a high grade of rock are good. Then the rock itself must be tested.

In testing, a number of holes are drilled at various spots in the area. Special drills are used that can cut a core of rock about two inches in diameter. This core is brought up to the surface and analyzed. Some drills can go down as far as two thousand eight hundred feet, or more than half a mile. The test indicates whether there is enough good stone available to make quarrying profitable.

HOW MANY TYPES OF CLIMATE ARE THERE?

There are many different types of climate on earth. Climate, by the way, is the combination of temperature, moisture, wind, and sunshine at a place over a period of many years. Climates of the world can be classified according to their latitudes and the plants that grow there. Different kinds of plants need different amounts of moisture and heat to grow. So the vegetation of a place tells us about temperature and rainfall conditions over a long period of time.

Basically, there are five major classifications of climates, with many subdivisions in each class. There are tropical climates, subtropical climates, mid-latitude climates, high-latitude climates, and high-altitude climates.

Tropical climates are found in regions between 350° North and 350° South latitude. In the tropical rain forests (nearest the Equator), conditions are warm and rainy all year long, and there is a thick cover of trees. In this tropical area there are also tropical wet-and-dry climates; tropical savannas, where the climate is too dry for forests; tropical steppes (still drier); and the tropical desert climate.

Subtropical climates prevail in 30° and 40° North and South latitudes. In these areas there is a Mediterranean climate of hot, dry summers and mild, wet winters and a humid subtropical climate of hot summers and mild winters, with enough rainfall in all seasons to sustain forests.

Mid-latitude climates occur between 40° and 60° North and South latitudes. Included in this area are a marine west coast climate (west coast of North America); cool steppe or cool desert climates; and humid continental climates—each with different vegetation and rainfall patterns.

High-latitude climates are characteristic of from 60° North and South latitudes to the Poles. Here temperatures are very cold in winter and cool in summer. Within this area is a taiga climate (very cold in winter); a tundra climate, where only grasses, mosses and lichens can grow; and the polar climate, where great ice caps exist.

High-altitude climates, or highland climates, are found on the high mountains of the world, even at the Equator.

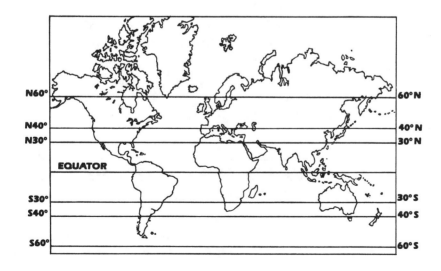

WHAT ARE OATS?

Oats are the seeds of a plant belonging to the grass family. When you think of oats, you probably think of the breakfast cereal called oatmeal or of oatmeal cookies. These are the only forms in which most people eat oats. What happens to the rest of the huge crop of oats? Most of it is used for animal food.

The first oats probably originated in the cool, moist areas of eastern Europe. For centuries men considered oats to be a weed. Some experts believe that the early Greeks and Romans cultivated oats for animal food. But it wasn't until the thirteenth century that peasants began to depend on oats as one of the most important foods for people.

Oats were brought to some small islands off New England in 1602 and spread rapidly as a crop in North America during the next fifty years. Today the United States is the biggest producer of oats, with Canada, the Soviet Union, and countries of northern Europe also producing great quantities.

Oat plants grow from two to five feet tall. The leaves are long and slender. Each stem has a head with many small, delicate branches. The branches end with little spikes on which the flowers blossom and the grains later form.

The plants grow in cool, moist climates. Oats do not need special soils, and as long as the land is not too wet, will often grow in places where other crops cannot be grown at all.

More than other cereal crops, oats are used as a general-purpose feed for animals. Harvested oats, mixed with other cereal grains, are used for all livestock and poultry.

When oats are milled for people to eat, the hard outer covering, or hull, and its parts are removed. The germ and other parts that are very rich in vitamins and minerals are left in.

WHAT IS THE DIFFERENCE BETWEEN FRUITS AND VEGETABLES?

The word "fruit" usually describes any fleshy part of a plant that has developed from a flower and has seeds. Vegetables are herbaceous plants. An herbaceous plant is one that has a soft stem and little or no woody tissue.

According to botanists, the part of a plant that carries seeds is its fruit. They divide fruits into three main classes: fleshy fruits with seeds in the flesh, such as oranges, melons, berries, and apples; fruits containing pits or stones, such as cherries, plums, and peaches; and dry fruits, such as nuts, grains, beans, and peas.

If it surprises you to learn that botanists consider beans and peas fruits (because they contain seeds), you will be even more surprised to learn that cucumbers and squash can be called fruits also! It all depends on how technical we want to be. In addition, because eating customs vary in different parts of the world, the same edible part of a plant may be considered a fruit in one place and a vegetable in another.

Just as there are "families" of related creatures in the animal kingdom, so many vegetables are related. Did you know, for example, that the cabbage, turnip, radish, broccoli, and cauliflower all belong to one family of vegetables?

Lettuce, chicory, and artichokes belong to another vegetable family. The gourd family includes cucumbers, melons, pumpkins, and squash. The pea family consists of peas, all kinds of beans, peanuts, and soybeans.

Asparagus is related to the common onion, leek, garlic, chive and shallot. Beets, spinach, and Swiss chard all belong to one family. And here is an interesting one: the nightshade family. It includes potatoes, eggplants, peppers, and tobacco!

Fruits and vegetables are alike in that they supply us with the vitamins and minerals that help to keep us healthy.

IS THE TOMATO A FRUIT OR A VEGETABLE?

Of course, it doesn't really matter very much which it is, since we use it in this country as a vegetable. A fascinating thing about this question is that the Supreme Court of the United States actually had to decide what the tomato is!

Botanically, the tomato is a fruit. There can be no question about that. But it is used in soups, sauces, ketchup, and in many other ways in the main part of the meal. So, for purposes of trade, the Supreme Court in 1893 classified the tomato as a vegetable!

The tomato originated in its wild form in South America in Peru, Ecuador, and Bolivia. Long before Columbus came to the new world, cultivated forms of the tomato had already been developed in Mexico. And it is probable that tomatoes from Mexico were the first ones ever seen by people in Europe.

The first definite description of the tomato in Europe was in Italy in 1554, where it was called *pomi d'oro,* or "apple of gold." This means that a yellow type of tomato was the first kind known in Europe. Before the end of the sixteenth century, tomatoes were being grown in the gardens of England, Spain, Italy, France and the countries of mid-Europe. But they were considered a sort of curiosity.

By the mid-1700's people in several countries of Europe were using the tomato as food, and the first person to grow it in the United States was Thomas Jefferson, in 1781. But a great many people considered the tomato to be poisonous. It wasn't until about 1900 that it became popular for eating.

The tomato plant is a relative of the potato and tobacco plants. It needs a long growing season and light, rich, well-drained soil. In northern Europe and the northern United States it is often grown in hothouses during the winter. It is also grown in Florida, Texas, and Mexico during the winter. Winter tomatoes are picked while green and shipped to northern markets. They ripen on the way to market.

HOW IS TOBACCO GROWN?

The tobacco plant usually grows four to six feet high. The leaves are large, about two or three feet in length. They are covered with many long, soft hairs that hold a gummy juice.

There are many ways in which this plant is grown, but all commercial tobacco needs a lot of care. Tobacco seed is mixed with fertilizer and corn or cottonseed meal before it is sown. In warm areas, the seedbeds are covered with cotton cloth. In colder areas the covering is usually glass.

In six to ten weeks in most areas, the plants grow six to eight inches. They develop four to six leaves, and are now ready to be set into fields that have been carefully prepared and fertilized.

As the plants begin to flower, each is topped, which means that the budding seed head is removed. This is done so that the leaves will be stronger and have a deeper color.

Three or four months after the seedlings have been placed in the growing field, the plants are ready for harvesting. Two methods are used: priming and stalk cutting.

In priming tobacco, each leaf is pulled separately as it ripens. Two to four leaves are removed from a plant each week. This process takes five to eight weeks. In stalk-cut tobacco, the whole plant is cut down.

After harvesting, the tobacco must be cured. The purpose of this is to dry the leaf and bring out the proper color. A tobacco leaf is cured by heat, air, or sun. In flue-curing, green leaves are hung in small insulated barns that are heated by flues. Stalk-cut tobacco is air cured. Other types of tobacco are strung together on sticks and hung in the sun.

The final stage in the care of tobacco is aging. This is done to mellow the leaf and improve its flavor.

WHAT IS PAPRIKA?

True pepper is made from the pepper plant, which has the scientific name of *Piper nigrum*. But a great many other kinds of pepper are obtained from plants of entirely different families.

For example, there are the red pepper or chilies. They belong to the genus *capsicum*. There are also cayenne peppers and tabasco peppers. Still another kind, bell peppers, are called pimientos when canned in oil. Pimientos is the Spanish name for the pepper plant. And finally there is paprika, which is a red pepper produced from the bell pepper. When these are ripe, they are red and hot, but are milder than many other kinds. That's why paprika can be used more freely than other kinds of pepper.

Pepper is considered to be the most important of all the spices in the world. After salt, it is the seasoning most used for food. In ancient times, and during the middle ages, only the rich could afford to use pepper. It had to be carried by caravan from the Far East, and this made it so expensive that a pound of pepper was considered a fitting present for a king!

In some ways pepper was like gold. People could pay taxes with pepper, and it was given as tribute to rulers by their subjects. When an army conquered an enemy and soldiers were given a share of the spoils, pepper would be one of the great rewards they would receive.

The Portuguese were so anxious to find a way of getting pepper at lower cost that they tried to find a sea route to India. After they found the way around the Cape of Good Hope, the cost of pepper in Europe dropped a great deal. Today, of course, pepper costs so little that we don't even think twice when we buy it. In the United States, more than fifteen thousand tons of pepper are used a year!

Pepper comes from the fruit or seeds of a climbing shrub. Black pepper is made by picking unripe berries and drying them until black. White pepper is made by removing the outer coat before grinding.

WHAT IS A HYBRID PLANT?

First of all, what is a hybrid? A hybrid is a crossbreed of a plant or animal. This means that it is the result of the union of the male of one species, race, etc., with the female of another.

This can happen in nature or among people without any deliberate plan. But in plants this is often done deliberately and for very good reasons.

Probably the best example of the advantages of hybrid plants is the case of corn. In the early days in the United States, farmers took particular care in the selection of seed ears for the next year's crop. By constant selection many varieties and strains of corn thus came into existence. These were selected because of their adaptability to different soils and climates.

But beginning about 1905, plant scientists started a new method of producing different kinds of corn. It was discovered that when the plant was self-pollinated—that is, the pollen in the tassels was applied by hand to the silks on the ear of the same plant—widely different kinds of corn plants appeared. By repeating this process and saving only the best plants for seed strains, "inbred lines" were established.

Many of these inbred lines had certain special, desirable characteristics, but all of them were lower in yield. Now came the next step. When such inbred lines were cross-pollinated, by applying the pollen of one strain to the silks of another, the kernels thus formed often gave rise to very productive hybrid plants.

And these hybrid plants were very good indeed! In many cases they were superior in disease resistance and in strength of stalks, and were very high in yield. Thus by first purifying or sorting out the most desirable characters of the old varieties, and then recombining these, very superior types of corn have been produced. In other plants, too, the same process of producing hybrids has had wonderful results!

WHAT IS A SPORE?

A flowering plant makes a new plant by means of a seed. Plants that don't have flowers make a new plant by means of a spore.

A spore is a one-celled organism. It is invisible to the eye and can only be seen under a microscope. There are spores in the air all around us. That's why when food is left exposed, and molds and mildews form on it, we know where they came from. Some types of spores that were in the air settled on the food and began to grow.

Some of the plants that reproduce by means of spores are mushrooms, ferns, and mosses. The algae that live in water also produce spores.

A plant carries its spores in cases that are called sporangia. In a mushroom, the sporangium is inside the gills beneath the mushroom cap. In mosses, the spores are carried in a capsule at the top of the stalk.

When the spore case is ripe, it opens, and the ripe spores are released. Since they are finer than dust, the wind scatters them far and wide. In the case of water plants, such as the algae, the spores can actually swim away. They have tiny tails called cilia. These spores are called zoospores, and when the ripe case opens, the zoospores swim away quickly. After a short time they come to rest and lose their tails. Then they begin to grow into new plants.

Some spores reproduce by cell division. They grow by pushing out a germ tube through a thin place in the cell wall. The germ tube branches into a mass of threads out of which the new plant grows. This is called asexual reproduction, because differentiated male and female cells are not needed for reproduction to take place.

Other spores are specialized male and female cells. In order to start a new plant, one male and one female cell must join to form a fertilized egg. Some plants alternate in the kind of spores they produce, asexual in one generation and sexual spores in the next.

DO CACTI HAVE LEAVES?

A cactus (plural: cacti) is able to exist under extreme conditions because it is a plant that has adapted itself to those conditions.

Cacti have the same basic structures and processes as other plants. But the work that is done by leaves in most other plants is done by the stems and branches of the cacti. In fact, the absence of leaves and the presence of spine-covered branches and stems enable them to survive in hot, dry regions.

The leaves of other plants are thin structures and are filled with pores through which the plant breathes. During the cell-making process carried on by the plants, water is given off to the air through these pores.

A cactus plant must guard every drop of water. So the work of the leaves is taken over by the stems and branches. Their thick skins have very few pores, and the water in the cactus is retained.

The roots of cacti are spread out, close to the surface of the ground. That's why cacti can quickly absorb water from the earth after

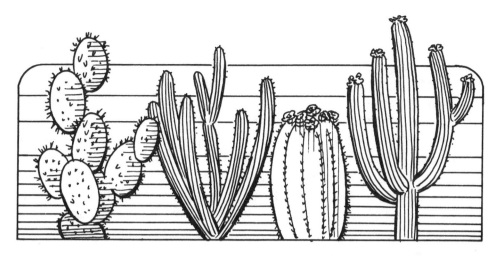

a rainfall. This water, which is taken in through the roots, is stored in the spongy or hollow stems of a cactus. The outer layer of the plant is thick and waxy, and this also prevents the escape of water.

The outer skin of a cactus is ribbed. Some cacti have ribs that fold and expand like an accordion. They expand as they fill up with water and fold together as the water in the stem is used up.

There are some members of the cactus family that do have leaves, such as the lemon vine of the West Indies. But in most cacti the leaves have developed into spines, needles, or hairs. These help protect the cacti from animals that would otherwise eat them, since they may be the only green plants in the area.

WHAT IS A NATIONAL FOREST?

National forests are areas that belong to all the people of the United States. They are protected and managed, along with the national grasslands, by the Forest Service of the United States Department of Agriculture.

To most people the word "forest" means trees. And it is true that the national forests are the source of much of the nation's timber. But they are much more than this. Many of them contain grazing lands that have few trees. Some parts of the national-forest system have been set aside as wilderness areas. No cutting of trees is allowed there, there are no structures to spoil the scenery, and no machines are allowed to disturb the peace and quiet.

The national forests are also the home of more than one-third of the country's big-game animals and of many millions of smaller creatures. Lakes cover nearly two million acres. Skiing areas are used by winter-sports fans. Areas large enough for almost three hundred thousand persons to camp in at one time are maintained, and there are eighty-one thousand miles of fishing streams.

More than one hundred million people visit the national forests each year. In the 154 national forests and nineteen national grasslands, there is a total of 186,000,000 acres. Most of these lands have always been owned by the public. In the eastern United States, however, much national-forest land was specially purchased by the government to protect the watersheds of streams, to produce timber, and to provide for recreation.

National forests differ from national parks. National parks have been set aside to preserve in a natural state some outstanding examples of America's scenic and scientific treasures. In the national parks no hunting, cutting of timber, or other removal of resources is permitted.

WHAT ARE HARDWOODS AND SOFTWOODS?

Trees, and the woods that come from them, have been divided into two main classes. The common name for one class of trees and lumber is softwoods, and the other class is called hardwoods. The difference between them is supposed to be in their hardness or softness of texture. A harder wood, as you might imagine, doesn't scratch as easily and stands up better under wear and tear.

The most important North American softwoods are the cedar, southern cypress, Douglas fir, true fir, hemlock, western larch, northern white pine, ponderosa pine, southern pine, sugar pine, western white pine, redwood, and spruce. Softwoods are also described in terms of being evergreens, cone-bearing trees, or needle-leaved trees.

Hardwood trees generally have broad leaves and shed them in the autumn or in the spring, as some oaks do. The important North American hardwoods are the ash, aspen, basswood, beech, birch, cottonwood, elm, gum, hickory, maple, oak, black walnut, and yellow poplar.

But the terms "softwoods" and "hardwoods" are really used as names for a class of woods or trees. Some of the softwoods are really hard in texture, and some of the hardwoods are soft—softer than some of the so-called softwoods!

The "basic wood substance" of which the cell walls of all woods are made weighs about the same in all kinds of woods. But because the cells have cavities of various sizes, a greater or lesser portion of the wooden block is taken up by these cavities. The size and proportions of the openings and walls of the wood cells vary greatly. This is why there is so much difference in the weight of various woods. Oak, for example, weighs more than twice as much as basswood. The greater the weight, the stronger the wood.

WHAT IS JADE?

Jade is a gemstone that almost glows. It has been prized by man for thousands of years.

The Chinese language uses the same word to mean both "jade" and "precious stone." The English word "jade" comes from the Spanish *piedra de ijada,* which means "colic stone." The Spanish called it this because they believed jade cured stomach pains!

Jade can be either of two separate minerals, jadeite or nephrite. These look so much alike that only an expert can tell them apart. Jadeite is slightly harder than nephrite. It also has a translucent glow and comes in more colors.

Jade is white in its pure state, but enough mineral impurities are usually present to make jade bright yellow, red, or one of the many shades of green. The most desired shade of jade is an emerald-green, or "Imperial" jade, which may be almost transparent. This type comes from Burma.

Because jade is a tough and hard stone, primitive men used it to make axes, hammers, knives, and other useful tools. Later, men used it for bowls, carvings, jewelry, and charms.

Jade is so tough that it is very difficult to carve. Steel chisels will not work. So instead, gritty materials are rubbed over the surface until it wears away. Making a simple vase may take two or three years of work.

Carved jade pieces have been found in Mexico that are at least three thousand five hundred years old. The early men of Central America used some jade in tools, but used it mostly for religious purposes. The Aztecs considered jade to be worth many times its weight in gold.

China is the country where jade has been of the greatest importance. For three thousand years the Chinese have been making lovely jade carvings. The Chinese admire jade so much that those who can afford it always carry small pieces with them. They believe that when jade is fingered, some of its secret virtues rub off.

WHAT IS A FUEL?

A fuel is a material that is burned in order to get heat and light, and also to generate power. The process of burning, or combustion, is a chemical reaction. A material combines with oxygen from the air and gives off energy. The energy is given off in the form of heat and light.

The energy in fuels came originally from the sun. The plants from which fuels come trap energy from the sun's rays and use it to build their tissues. Burning wood and charcoal releases energy that has been stored up by plants in this way. When we burn coal or oil, we use energy stored up by plants that lived millions of years ago.

There are many different types of fuels, and actually anything that burns can be called a fuel. But the most common fuels are wood, coal, natural gas, and gasoline.

Fuels can also be classified as solid, liquid, or gaseous. Or they can be classified according to their origin—natural, chemical, or metal based.

Wood was one of the first fuels used by man, and was his most important one for many centuries. It was the easiest to get, and the cheapest. But during the sixteenth century, wood started to become scarce in Europe, and coal began to replace it.

Coal contains a high percentage of carbon. Carbon is the most important part of most fuels. Fuels with a high percentage of carbon burn evenly and with a hot flame. Hard coal, or anthracite, has a higher percentage of carbon than other types of coal, and so makes less smoke and ash.

The most important liquid fuels come from petroleum. They include kerosene, gasoline, and heating oils.

34

WHAT IS NATURAL GAS?

In certain parts of Iran and India, where natural gas issued from crevices in the rocks, the natives thought their fire god was responsible for it. So they kept it burning as a tribute to him.

The curious thing is that in the United States, which seems to have the greatest accumulation of natural gas, people didn't know what it was either for a long time, and didn't know what to do with it. Since natural gas sometimes escapes from rocks or crevices without any drilling, these places were called "burning springs" in the United States as early as 1775. The first discovery of gas by drilling was made in the nineteenth century. It wasn't collected and piped on a commercial scale until 1872.

Natural gas is a mixture of combustible gases and vapors, chiefly methane. Sometimes it is found alone; sometimes it is found mixed with oil and must be extracted. At other places it is found with oil but is not mixed with it.

In nearly every oil field there is natural gas. It gathers in porous rock with a covering of heavy shale that keeps the gas in and keeps the air out. It accumulates in a kind of arched section of the stone, and sometimes there are gas beds above the oil.

When drilling is carried on at oil fields and oil is brought in, it sometimes happens that a gas bed is tapped, too, and gas begins to escape in a great flame. At one oil field in Oklahoma, about $25,000 worth of oil a day was collected, but at the same time $75,000 worth of gas escaped every day for a whole year!

Natural gas is clean and convenient to use for cooking and heating, but because of the problem of transportation it costs more than coal in most places. Today there are great pipeline systems that carry natural gas from its source to far distant places in a network that covers the country. In some cases the natural gas is carried through these pipes for more than one thousand miles!

WHAT IS A CORAL REEF?

Let's start by finding out what coral is. A chunk of coral is made of the skeletons of tiny marine animals called coral polyps.

The polyp's skeleton grows outside its body. It is cup-shaped, and it protects and supports the polyp's body and grows as the animal grows. When the polyp dies, the skeleton is left. Coral reefs and islands are formed of billions upon billions of these tiny skeletons.

A coral colony consists of living corals. Each is attached to a solid base, such as a rock or the skeletons of earlier generations of corals. Coral colonies are found in all the seas, but reef-building coral polyps are found only in warm, shallow waters. A depth of about 150 feet is best for them. Yet in some parts of the world coral reefs rise from great ocean depths.

The mystery of how coral reefs were formed was solved by Charles Darwin, the famous naturalist. Darwin knew that the earth's surface changes. Mountains are forced up in one place; in another, the crust of the earth sinks.

When he was studying coral reefs, he noticed that there were three kinds: fringing reefs, barrier reefs, and atolls (rings of coral). Putting all this information together, he worked out the following theory:

A volcanic island forms where an undersea volcano rises above the surface of the water. In the shallow waters of the island shores, corals build a fringing reef. As time passes, the volcano becomes cold and dead; it begins to sink back into the sea. As a result the fringing reef now becomes separated from the island by a wider channel of water, and it goes on growing. It has become a barrier reef.

If the volcano sinks completely and vanishes, only the coral reef is left; it has become an atoll, a ring of coral surrounding a lagoon. In addition, we know today that island shores may rise or sink, and ocean levels may rise or fall. All these changes help explain the building of coral reefs.

HOW ARE SEASHELLS FORMED?

If you've ever walked along a beach, you've probably seen a seashell lying on the sand where it has been washed in by the waves. The shell will nearly always be empty, for it is the home of some sea animal that has died.

By the way, shells are also found in woodlands, rivers, and ponds as well as the sea. When people speak of shells, they usually mean those of soft-bodied animals known as mollusks.

Most mollusks have shells outside their soft bodies. The shell is a mollusk's skeleton. It is part of the animal and the mollusk is attached to it by muscles. The soft animal inside can never leave its shell and return to it. As the mollusk grows bigger, its shell increases in size and strength.

The shell is made of a form of limestone and is built by the mollusk itself. Certain glands in the mollusk are able to take limestone from the water and deposit it in tiny particles at the edge of, and along the inside of, the shell. As a mollusk grows in size, its shell increases in thickness and size. You can see the lines of growth that are marked by ridges that run parallel to the outer edge. You've probably noticed these growth lines in the shells of oysters and clams. The other ridges are caused by ridges in the "mantle" of the mollusk, or by muscles in its body.

The shell of a mollusk consists of three layers. The outside is covered with a thin layer of hornlike material that contains no lime. Under this is a layer of carbonate of lime. The inside layer is the "mother-of-pearl," or nacre. It is made up of very thin alternate layers of carbonate of lime and a horny substance.

The coloring of the shell comes from some glands of the mollusk that contain coloring matter. So a shell may be spotted, all one color, or marked with lines. Some shells are so tiny they can only be seen with a magnifying glass, while the giant clam has a shell that can be four feet long.

DOES SEAWEED HAVE ANY USE?

All over the world wherever there is a body of sea water, there seaweed may be found. Seaweed occurs in many varieties. It belongs to a large group of water plants called algae—plants without true leaves, stems, roots, or flowers.

But they do contain a green pigment called chlorophyll. Therefore, they are capable of making their own food. The reason these plants don't look green is that the chlorophyll is often concealed by other pigments. So some seaweed looks brown or red.

In the Temperate Zone, the most common seaweeds belong to the brown algae. This is the seaweed that grows between the high and low-tide lines. It has bubblelike floats that children enjoy crackling open between their fingers. The plants are attached to rocks by means of rootlike holdfasts.

Another well-known form of seaweed is the kelp. It has various forms. Most commonly they are long, flat, tough, bladelike forms that fasten to rocks by means of leathery stalks. Some of these seaweeds along the Atlantic Coast grow as long as twenty feet, and the giant kelp of the Pacific Ocean is even longer!

These kelp are among the seaweeds that are useful to man. They are often used as fertilizer because they have a high concentration of potash. They are also a source of iodine.

Another useful kind of seaweed is called Irish moss. It is rather rough and leathery in form. It produces a great deal of agar, which is a colorless substance resembling jelly. In the Orient, tons of seaweed belonging to the red-algae group are dried and used as food! They are not very nourishing, but contain a great deal of agar. They are used in thickening soups and providing bulk in other foods.

Seaweed is also a primary source of food for ocean life. Smaller sea creatures feed on it, and they in turn become food for the larger ones. Seaweed gives off oxygen, and this helps to keep the water pure. So you see why seaweed is considered quite useful to man.

WHAT IS THE CONTINENTAL SHELF?

When you think of the Atlantic Ocean, you think of the top surface of the water. But what is under the water, at the bottom of the ocean floor? Let's imagine that we are making a voyage out of New York, due east across the Atlantic Ocean. Here is a picture of the bottom as we move across the ocean.

For about two hundred miles, the bottom gradually slopes down. It is generally flat, but occasionally there is a V-shaped valley or canyon. This is the continental shelf. The continental shelf is part of the North American continent. It just happens to be too low to stand out of the sea.

At the depth of about one thousand two hundred feet, the shelf suddenly comes to an end. It is no longer gently sloping but there is a steep incline. This is the continental edge or slope, and it goes down to the full depth of the ocean.

Moving along past the slope, the ocean depth is about two-and-a-half miles. We are now crossing the deep ocean. Here the ocean bottom is very flat. It is called an abyssal plain. Abyssal plains cover about a third of the sea floor and are among the flattest places found on earth.

As we keep on moving across the ocean, we reach an area where there are humps on the sea floor. Some are the size of hills. This is called the Mid-Atlantic ridge. Near the center of the ridge the hills are higher and steeper, and some rise like mountains to within five thousand feet of the surface.

Between the mountains are deep valleys with flat floors. Right in the middle of the ridge lies the largest valley of all. It is called the mid-ocean rift. The rift is like a crack between the two halves of the ridge.

As we continue eastward, we again cross an abyssal plain. The plain slopes gently upward to the continental shelf off Portugal. And this is a picture of the bottom of the Atlantic Ocean.

WHAT IS A MARINE BIOLOGIST?

A marine biologist studies the creatures that live in the sea. To do this he has to catch fishes and study them when they are dead. Or else he must go down in the water and watch them while they are alive.

One of the most important tools of the biologist is the pickling bottle, containing alcohol or formalin. Without it he would have very little time to look at a creature he has collected, for the animal would soon decay.

Besides the pickling bottle the marine biologist uses a trawl net to catch fishes and other sea creatures. The trawl net is cone-shaped and looks something like a butterfly net. Its mouth is sewn to a hoop, and the rest trails behind. A towline from a ship is attached to the hoop. A heavy weight pulls down the line as the ship sails along.

Water and fishes flow in through the mouth of the net. The water escapes, but the fishes are caught. To catch bigger and fast-swimming fishes, the net is made with large meshes so that the water can flow through easily and the trawl can be towed very fast. To catch smaller fishes, the meshes are made finer.

When the biologist feels that enough has been caught, the net is hauled in. It is tipped out onto a canvas. The various kinds of creatures are counted, and the ones to be kept are popped into their bottles. What is left is thrown back or sent to the ship's galley.

Sometimes color pictures are taken of the specimens minutes after they die. This is done because many dead fish lose their color very quickly, even when they are preserved.

Back in the laboratory, the specimens are dissected. This means that they are carefully taken apart in order to examine every part of their bodies. The biologist dissects to learn how creatures are built. Then he can determine their differences and similarities.

WHAT IS ANTHROPOLOGY?

Like most sciences, the name of this one tells you what it is about. The name anthropology comes from two Greek words: *anthropos,* meaning "man," and *logos,* meaning "science." So anthropology should mean the study of man.

In a large sense, that is what anthropology is concerned with: man's physical structure, his customs and habits, his languages, arts and religions, and his civilizations. This means that a great many other studies are very closely linked with anthropology—for example, anatomy, physiology, psychology, ethics, sociology, and so on.

But, in actual practice, anthropology limits itself to a much narrower field. You might say that for practical purposes, three studies make up anthropology. The first is the study of man's place in nature. What separates man from other animals? What characteristics of his body set him apart from monkeys and other animals? How does his skull compare with that of a chimpanzee? The purpose of such studies is to trace the connection between man's physical qualities and his development and civilization.

The next study anthropology is concerned with is the various races of man and their classification. This is called ethnology. This science deals with the physical differences between the various human races. It compares the skeletons and skulls of prehistoric man with those of modern man. It also deals with the customs and religions of various tribes and peoples to find out how races differ and how they develop.

There is a third, a special branch of anthropology, called anthropometry. This is the science that deals with the physical measurements of man, the height and weight of various races, the shape of their bones, and so on.

WHAT IS THE SPHINX?

Of course, the sphinx most of us think of is the Great Sphinx that stands at Giza, Egypt, near the pyramids. Actually, a sphinx is a monster that was common in the myths of ancient peoples. The Greeks thought of it as having the head of a woman, the body of a lion, and wings. The Egyptians thought of it as a wingless lion with the head and breast of a man.

The Great Sphinx of Egypt was once a hill of rock left over from the building of the Great Pyramid. Later it was carved into a huge lion with the head of a man. It stands 66 feet high with a length of 240 feet. It was probably carved to resemble the face of a king called Chephren, a king of the fourth Egyptian dynasty.

In ancient times, lions lived in the desert just beyond the valley of the Nile. Because they were strong and beautiful, Egyptian sculptors carved statues of them to guard the entrances to temples. Later on, instead of a lion's head, they carved the head of a king.

In ancient Egypt the kings were considered to be descended from the sun god, who was called Ra. When a king died, he himself was supposed to become the sun god. So the Great Sphinx represents the king as the sun god guarding the pyramids.

Although there is no other sphinx as large as the Great Sphinx at Giza, many kings had their likenesses carved as sphinxes. In one case, a sphinx was made with the face of a woman, Queen Hatshepsut, who seized the throne and ruled the country. This sphinx was given a beard to represent Queen Hatshepsut's power.

WHY IS A FOUR-LEAF CLOVER LUCKY?

The desire of man to protect himself from unknown forces, or to create good fortune for himself, has led to thousands upon thousands of superstitions the world over. In fact, we can roughly divide superstitions into those that are supposed to bring good luck and those that are supposed to bring bad luck.

The four-leaf clover is believed by people all over the world to be a sign of coming good fortune and happiness. It is such an old superstition that no one can say exactly how or where it began. But there is an old legend about it that some people believe. The legend is that when Eve was sent away from Paradise, she took a four-leaf clover with her. Because the clover was a bit of green from the Garden of Paradise, it came to be considered an omen of good luck if found in one's own garden!

Just as widespread, and just as hard to explain, is the common belief that a horseshoe is lucky. Almost every country has a different legend or tradition concerning the horseshoe. The Irish say that the horse was in the stable where Christ was born, and therefore the horseshoe has magical power. In Russia, the blacksmith used to be considered a kind of magician, and it is claimed he used the horseshoe as a charm in performing his magic. Even the ancient Romans believed

that finding a cast-off horseshoe in the road would protect one from illness. This may be because iron at one time was regarded as a good-luck charm.

When it comes to bad-luck omens, the fear of a black cat is one of the oldest. In the Middle Ages, when people believed in witches, it was assumed that witches and evil spirits took the form of the black cat. Today, many people are still uneasy to see a black cat cross their path!

The broken mirror is another bad-luck superstition that goes back to ancient times. In ancient Greece it was believed that one saw the will of the gods in the mirror. Therefore, if a mirror was broken accidentally, it meant that the gods didn't want the person to see the future because it held unpleasant things!

The Romans believed that a person's health changed every seven years. Since the mirror reflected the health of a person, they thought that breaking a mirror meant that the health of a person would be broken for seven years!

WHAT IS THE ROSETTA STONE?

As you know, one of the greatest civilizations of all time was the one of ancient Egypt. A long time ago, man had already begun to unearth monuments and buildings and treasures of all sorts going back to ancient Egypt. There was a strange kind of writing found with many of these objects and buildings, but no one could read it. And there seemed to be no way to figure out what it meant.

The early Greeks believed that Egyptian priests produced these writings for sacred purposes, so they called them *hieroglyphs,* which meant "sacred carvings." And this type of writing came to be known as hieroglyphics.

After the Greeks, no big effort was made to understand these writings until the seventeenth century, when many scholars worked on the problem. But they had no success. Then in 1799, a wonderful discovery was made. A black slab of basalt was found, which had lain for centuries near one of the mouths of the river Nile. It was named the Rosetta stone after the town where it was found.

Now what made the Rosetta stone so valuable was that it had a message written in three different languages. One was Greek; a second, hieroglyphics; and the third, a late form of Egyptian writing called demotic, a sort of abbreviated hieroglyphic.

Many years of study of these writings now began. The Greek text could be read and understood, and by comparing it to the others the long-lost secret of hieroglyphic writing was finally revealed. The man who accomplished this in 1822 was a brilliant young Frenchman called Jean François Champollion.

As a result of his discovery, it has been possible for historians to trace the life, customs, and religion of the Egyptians as far back as 3500 B.C. This was because hieroglyphics were the earliest form of Egyptian writing and one of the oldest-known systems of writing.

Basically it is picture writing. Each picture represents an object. But this writing developed as time went on, and later Egyptians wrote down words and ideas and sounds.

WHO WERE THE KNIGHTS?

Knights were the highest class of fighting men in Europe during the Middle Ages. The knights, who fought on horseback, were the aristocrats of the battlefield.

Their whole way of life was based on warfare, and they were the great heroes of that time. The high position of the knights was partly due to the fact that during the early Middle Ages kings and governments had very little real authority. Power belonged to the best fighters. The man who had horses and heavy arms and knew how to use them had a great advantage.

From their walled and moated castles the more powerful knights ruled the nearby countryside. They honored no law but their own, and they freely made war against their neighbors. A knight did as he wished, because no one else was powerful enough to stop him. Many knights did keep some sort of order in their land and protected their people from bandits. But many a knight was no better than a bandit himself.

The warfare of the knights was like a game, and their games were like war. The sport that was most like battle was the tournament. In time, tournaments became mock battles in which knights fought with flattened lances and blunted swords. The object of a tournament was about the same as that of a battle—to capture an enemy and collect ransom.

Knights had rules of behavior, called the code of chivalry. A knight was supposed to treat his captive as an honored guest, even if they had been bitter enemies. One knight was not supposed to attack another without warning.

Knights observed this chivalry among themselves because it was a matter of mutual advantage. A knight might be captured by another knight someday.

Knights could be attacked without warning, so no knight left his castle without wearing his heavy, uncomfortable armor for protection.

HOW OLD WAS JOAN OF ARC?

Saint Joan of Arc is honored by the people of France as one of their greatest heroines. She was born on January 6, 1412, and was burned at the stake on May 30, 1431. So she was only nineteen years old when she died.

When Joan was very young, much of France was ruled by the Burgundians, a powerful group of nobles who had joined with the English to gain control of the country.

When Joan was about thirteen years old, she began to hear "voices," which she said were those of Saints Catherine and Margaret, and of Michael the Archangel. She said the voices told her that she must bring peace to France by having the Dauphin Charles, who was heir to the throne, crowned king.

In time, Joan convinced Charles that she could lead his troops to victory. Joan inspired the French soldiers; they defeated the English, and the Dauphin was crowned Charles VII.

Later on, the king didn't give her full support in her efforts to continue the fight, the French troops began to suffer losses, and Joan was captured by the Burgundians.

She was accused of being a witch. Her judges were French clergymen who supported the Burgundians and English. During her trial, Joan behaved with great bravery. But she was found guilty and sentenced to death.

In 1455 a new court judged that she had been wrongly executed. The Catholic Church declared Joan a saint in 1920, and celebrates her feast on the anniversary of her death, May 30.

The story of Joan of Arc has become one of the most inspiring in history, and many books, plays, and ballads have been written about her.

WHO WAS NAPOLEON?

Few men in history have had as great an influence on the world and the times in which they lived as Napoleon Bonaparte.

He was born on August 15, 1769, in Ajaccio on the island of Corsica. When he was a boy, he identified himself with the great heroes of ancient history whom he read about. He was barely sixteen years old when he graduated from the military academy in Paris.

When he was just twenty-four years old, he was promoted to brigadier general for helping recapture the city of Toulon from the British. Later he led armies to victory over Austria, and won a war in Egypt.

Napoleon became the first consul, the ruler of France. He reformed the whole structure of government, enacting the Code Napoleon, which became the basis of modern French law.

In 1804, Napoleon was proclaimed emperor of France. During the ten years of the French Empire under Napoleon, there was almost continuous war. But his victories enabled him to dominate Europe from Spain to the borders of Russia.

In 1812 he decided to invade Russia with an army of more than six hundred thousand men. Even though he captured Moscow, his army didn't have enough supplies, so had to retreat. Only about one hundred thousand men survived the march home.

After several other defeats, Napoleon abdicated and was sent into exile on the island of Elba. He escaped from Elba and gathered a new army, but lost the battle at Waterloo to an allied army.

Napoleon surrendered to the British, who sent him as a prisoner to the barren island of St. Helena. There he remained until his death on May 5, 1821. While he led France to new greatness and power, it can also be said he caused great suffering and ruined the lives of whole nations of people.

WHO WAS LEONARDO DA VINCI?

Leonardo da Vinci was one of the most remarkable human beings who ever lived. Probably no one in history achieved so much in so many different fields as this man did.

Leonardo lived from 1452 to 1519. He was an outstanding painter, sculptor, and architect; he also designed bridges, highways, weapons, costumes, and scientific instruments. He invented the diving bell and tank and designed flying machines, though they could not be built with the materials of the time. He made important discoveries about the structure of the human body.

Leonardo approached science and art in the same methodical manner: After studying a problem, he made many sketches to help him find a solution. He saw no difference between planning a machine and a painting, and he became an expert in every field that interested him.

By the time Leonardo was twenty years old, he was listed as a master of the painters' guild. His work had a great influence on other painters, because he was always trying new things, such as the use of chiaroscuro, a technique which creates contrasts of light and dark.

One of Leonardo's greatest works, *The Last Supper,* was painted in Milan. Even though it is one of the world's masterpieces, it was actually an unsuccessful experiment. Because he worked slowly, Leonardo painted in oil on a damp wall. As a result, the painting began to peel, and today it is quite badly damaged.

Leonardo was interested in studying the human body, and he dissected corpses to find out how the body was put together. He also made many discoveries about plant growth.

Probably the single most famous painting in the world, the *Mona Lisa,* was painted by Leonardo in Florence.

WHO WAS SIR WALTER RALEIGH?

Almost everybody has heard the name of this man, but few people seem to know much about him. In the age of Elizabeth I, there were many great men, but Raleigh was probably the most varied in his genius and talents. He was soldier, sailor, courtier, poet, colonizer, historian, and scientist.

Raleigh was born about 1554 in Devonshire, England. As a youth he fought in the wars in France and later in Ireland. He won the favor of Queen Elizabeth I and was knighted and given various posts in the government.

Then Raleigh decided to do an interesting thing with the money he got from the Queen. He used it to start settlements in America. He sent out the first colony in 1585, a group of about one hundred men who lived on Roanoke Island, off the coast of North Carolina, for a year. This was the first English colony to experience life in the New World. All the later colonies flowed from this first attempt.

Much of our early knowledge of the Indians and of the geography of America and its plant and animal life we owe to Raleigh's efforts. In 1587 he sent out a second colony, but the colonists were all lost in the forests.

Raleigh knew many of the great poets and writers of his time, and he himself was one of the leading poets of his age. In 1595 he made his first voyage to Guiana in South America, where he hoped to find gold.

When King James I came to the throne, he accused Raleigh of being in a conspiracy against him and condemned him to death. Though the sentence was suspended, he spent most of the rest of his life in the Tower of London.

There he wrote a great book, *History of the World,* and made experiments in chemistry. In 1616 he was allowed out of prison and sailed again to Guiana. Instead of finding gold he clashed with the Spaniards and he was executed for this in 1618.

Raleigh was the man who introduced the potato from the New World to Ireland and was also the man who made smoking tobacco popular in Europe.

WHO WAS GEORGE WASHINGTON CARVER?

George Washington Carver was one of America's greatest agricultural scientists. His parents were the black slaves of a man called Moses Carver, who lived in Missouri. Soon after George was born, his father died. A few months later the baby and his mother were kidnapped by bandits. Moses Carver was able to buy George back, but his mother was never found, so the Carvers raised George themselves.

George showed a love for growing things at a very early age. He used to care for and cure sick plants, and the neighbors called him the plant doctor. He wandered about the United States seeking an education, doing all kinds of work to pay for his schooling. Finally he entered Iowa State College. He was the first black person to graduate from the college, and he became their first black teacher.

In 1896, he joined the staff of Tuskegee Institute, a new black college in Alabama. He was appointed to head the school's agriculture department. With the aid of his students, Carver built a homemade laboratory, using for equipment pots, kettles, and whatever else he could find that might be useful.

For nearly fifty years Carver taught at Tuskegee. In his laboratory he worked long hours, seeking ways to help the poor southern farmers. He introduced the peanut, pecan, and sweet potato to the cotton farmers, and showed them how these crops would enrich soil worn out by years of cotton planting.

In his laboratory he discovered new uses for these plants. From peanuts he made butter, coffee, ink, and soap. From sweet potatoes he made flour, cereals, glue, dyes, and rubber. He also made synthetic marble from wood shavings, rope from cornstalk fibers, and paint from Alabama clay.

Carver gave his discoveries to the world, asking no profit for himself. He gave advice freely to all who consulted him. He received offers of many high-paying jobs, but he preferred to remain at Tuskegee and teach. Today his great work is carried on through the George Washington Carver Foundation, which he set up with money from his savings. It provides scholarships for black students in agricultural research.

WHO WAS BOOKER T. WASHINGTON?

Booker Taliaferro Washington was one of America's great educators. He was born on a Virginia plantation on April 5, 1856. His mother was a slave who served as cook for the master's family.

After the Emancipation Proclamation was signed by Lincoln in 1863 freeing the slaves, Booker's mother left the plantation and moved with her children to Malden, West Virginia. There Booker entered a school for black children. To help support the family, he worked mornings in salt furnaces and coal mines before going to school.

At the age of seventeen, Booker entered the Hampton Normal and Agricultural Institute for black students in Virginia, and studied there for three years. After graduation he taught school and for awhile served as secretary to General Samuel Armstrong, principal of Hampton.

General Armstrong suggested Washington as organizer of a new industrial and teacher-training school for blacks in Tuskegee, Alabama. The school was very poor; no money was provided for buildings and land, and the first classes met in a run-down old church.

It was at Tuskegee that Washington did his great work as organizer and teacher. For years he traveled widely, sometimes by mule and buggy, to raise funds for the school. He was a stirring orator and made many speeches for the school. Washington was soon recognized as a leader in the field of Negro education.

During Washington's lifetime his school in Tuskegee grew until its campus consisted of over one hundred buildings, and its student body numbered almost one thousand six hundred. When he died in 1915, the school, now called Tuskegee Institute, remained as a monument to his life's work.

He was the author of several books. One of his best known is *Up From Slavery*.

WHAT IS THE DIFFERENCE BETWEEN A DEMOCRACY AND A REPUBLIC?

We in the United States live in both a democracy and a republic. A republic is a form of government that has no hereditary ruler, such as a king. But a republic need not be a democracy. A republic might have a dictator at the head of the government who holds all power, disregards the will of the people and doesn't allow the people to express their free choice.

On the other hand, a democracy might be a monarchy with a royal family, such as England has. England is one of the world's oldest and greatest democracies, even though it isn't a republic.

The word "democracy" comes from Greek and means the rule of the people. No nation can be considered democratic unless it gives protection to various human liberties. Among the democratic liberties are freedom of speech, movement, and association. The people must be free to express themselves on all issues and questions, and to move about as they please and associate with whom they choose.

Freedom of the press, religious freedom, and equality before the law are other democratic rights. It is very important in a democracy that life, liberty, and property be free from arbitrary and unlawful controls. Men of all races, religions, and degrees of wealth must be treated as equal before the law.

Such liberties are guaranteed by many nations in their constitutions. But such guarantees are not always upheld, and not every nation that claims it is a democracy really is.

Today, all over the world, the idea of democracy is being greatly expanded. It is believed by many that democracy should also include economic democracy, which means more equality in the wealth of men, and social equality, which means equality of opportunity to enjoy all the benefits of society, such as housing, health, and recreation.

HOW DID LAFAYETTE HELP THE UNITED STATES?

The Marquis de Lafayette, who was a brilliant leader in the French Revolution, also was a great fighter for the freedom of the American colonies.

He was born on September 6, 1757. At the age of thirteen he inherited a fortune so large that, in terms of today's money, he had an income of two million dollars a year. He was married at the age of sixteen.

In 1776 Lafayette decided to go to America to fight for the freedom of the colonies. Benjamin Franklin and other Americans in France encouraged his sympathy. Lafayette and a few companions reached Georgetown, South Carolina, on June 13, 1777. From Georgetown, Lafayette and his party traveled nine hundred miles overland, by coach and on horseback, to Philadelphia. There the Continental Congress gave him a commission as major general.

He first saw action at the battle of Brandywine, where he was wounded in the leg. He also went through the hardships of Valley Forge and fought at the Battle of Monmouth.

Lafayette then went back to France where he was able to arrange for six thousand French troops to be sent to America. He returned to bring General George Washington the good news.

Washington entrusted him with the defense of Virginia against the British. Lafayette successfully laid seige to the British Army under Lord Cornwallis. The British general had promised that he would capture "the boy." Instead, Lafayette was present at Yorktown on October 19, 1781, when Cornwallis surrendered. Then Lafayette, who knew that American independence was assured, returned to France. He was barely twenty-four years old.

When Lafayette died in Paris on May 20, 1834, flags in the United States were flown at half-mast, and the Army went into mourning for six months, as it had after George Washington's death.

WHAT IS A CATHEDRAL?

During the Middle Ages all of Western Europe was Roman Catholic. Each community had its own church. These churches were grouped into districts called dioceses. Each diocese was under the jurisdiction of a bishop.

The principal church of the diocese contained the throne of the bishop. In Latin the name of this church was *ecclesia cathedralis,* or "cathedral church." In English it has been shortened to "cathedral."

Most European cathedrals were constructed with the floor plan in the general shape of a cross. The long part of the cross is the nave and serves as the assembly room for the congregation.

The two arms of the cross are the transepts, and the fourth part, containing the altar and choir, is the apse. The section where the four parts meet is the crossing. Towers or domes were often built over the crossing.

Cathedrals have been built in nearly every style of architecture. But most of the very famous European cathedrals were either Byzantine, Romanesque, Gothic, or Renaissance.

Most of the very famous European cathedrals, such as Notre Dame of Paris, are in the Gothic style of the twelfth and thirteenth centuries. Strangely enough, the world's largest Gothic cathedral, St. John the Divine, was built in the nineteenth and twentieth centuries in New York City, and is not Roman Catholic, but Episcopal.

St. Peter's in Rome is not officially a cathedral, since it is not the seat of a bishop. It is an outstanding example of a Renaissance building. The dome was designed by the great Michelangelo, and is considered to be a masterpiece in itself.

WHAT WAS THE MONROE DOCTRINE?

Before and during the crisis over Cuba, there was much discussion of the Monroe Doctrine. The American Government said it had a right to keep European powers from trying to run the affairs of countries in the Western Hemisphere.

The Monroe Doctrine is a statement on foreign policy issued by President James Monroe. In December, 1823, he delivered a message to Congress, and part of it was devoted to foreign policy. This part came to be known as the Monroe Doctrine, and the foreign policy of the United States has been guided by it ever since. Here are the four main points included in this famous statement:

1. The American continents are not to be considered open to future colonization by any European powers.

2. The European political system is different from that of America. Any attempt to extend the European system to the Western Hemisphere will be considered dangerous to the peace and safety of the United States.

3. The United States will not interfere with any existing colonies or dependencies of European powers.

4. The United States has never taken any part in the internal affairs of European nations, nor will it do so in the future.

But for a long time the United States was not strong enough to enforce the Monroe Doctrine. For example, Napoleon III of France used French troops to place Archduke Maximilian of Austria upon the Mexican throne. But, in 1904, Theodore Roosevelt said that the United States could interfere in the affairs of Latin America to keep Europeans out, and United States Marines were sent into several countries during the next twenty years to restore order and protect the property of United States citizens.

Today the United States tries to uphold the Monroe Doctrine, but without interfering in the internal affairs of other American nations.

WHAT IS FASCISM?

Fascism is the name of a political movement founded by Benito Mussolini in Italy in 1919. Led by Mussolini, the Italian Fascists took over the government in 1922 and set up a one-party and one-man dictatorship that ruled Italy until 1943.

Similar movements in other countries, such as Hitler's Nazis in Germany, copied Mussolini's methods. The word "fascist" is used to describe all of these movements in general.

The fascists hated democracy. They believed ordinary people should not have the right to elect a government. Under fascism the "weak" were forced to obey the "strong." There was no political party but the fascist party.

The fascists had no use for justice or the rights of man. There were police and courts of law, but they were not there to protect the ordinary citizen. They were used to carry out the orders of the men in power.

The fascists had no use for freedom. People were forced to do what the state (which meant the fascists in control of the state) wanted them to do. The schools taught young people to obey and not to ask questions.

The fascist party controlled newspapers, books, and radio. They told editors and writers what to say and write. Nobody was allowed to write or say anything the fascists disliked.

The fascists had no use for peace. They wanted the nation to be strong and united so that it could go to war. They declared that a nation was only great if it made itself feared by others.

When Germany and Italy were defeated in World War II, fascism as a political philosophy and form of government was completely discredited.

WHAT IS EASTER?

Easter celebrates the Resurrection of Jesus Christ. It is the most important feast in the Christian calendar.

Easter Sunday does not come on the same date every year, but falls sometime between March 22 and April 25. It falls on the first Sunday after the first full moon following March 21, the vernal equinox (the time in spring when day and night are of equal length). The date of Easter Sunday was established by the church council of Nicaea in 325 A.D.

Easter Sunday ends a period of preparing for the feast of Easter. This forty-day period of prayer and fasting, called Lent, begins on Ash Wednesday and ends on Holy Saturday, the day before Easter. The Lenten fast commemorates Christ's forty-day fast in the desert.

The week from Palm Sunday to Easter Sunday is known as Holy Week. During Holy Week, church services remind one of the last days of Christ's life on earth. Palm Sunday marks Christ's entry into Jerusalem. Holy Thursday, also called Maundy Thursday, marks the Last Supper. Good Friday marks Christ's crucifixion, and Easter Sunday, his resurrection.

There are many customs that have developed around Easter. The custom of a sunrise service on Easter Sunday can be traced to ancient spring festivals that celebrated the rising sun. The new clothes worn on Easter Sunday are a symbol of new life. The custom comes from the baptism on Easter Sunday of early Christians, who were led into the church wearing new robes of white linen.

The familiar Easter parade goes back to the Middle Ages, when people walked about the countryside on Easter, stopping along the way to pray. Now, of course, it presents an opportunity for people to see and show their new spring clothes.

The egg is an Easter symbol, because it is a symbol of life. The Persians and Egyptians also colored eggs and ate them during their new year's celebration, which came in the spring.

IS NEW YEAR'S DAY THE SAME AROUND THE WORLD?

Welcoming the new year is one of the oldest and gayest customs celebrated the world over. But no festival has been observed on so many different dates or in so many different ways.

The ancient Greeks began their new year with the new moon after June 21. Before the time of Julius Caesar, the Roman new year started on March 1. In most European countries during the Middle Ages, the new year began on March 25.

What about today? In most Christian countries the new year begins on January 1. But other countries and religions observe New Year's Day on different dates, according to the calendars they use.

The Chinese celebrate two New Year's Days. One is on January 1, and the other takes place on the New Year's Day reckoned according to the Chinese lunar calendar. This may occur any time between January 21 and February 19.

Indonesia also has two New Year celebrations, one on January 1 and another on the Islamic New Year, a date that varies from year to year. The Russian Orthodox Church observes the New Year according to the Julian calendar, which places the day on January 14.

The Jewish New Year, Rosh Hashanah, is celebrated about the time of the autumnal equinox at the end of September or the beginning of October. In Vietnam the New Year usually begins in February.

Iran celebrates New Year's Day on March 21. Each of the religious groups in India has its own date for the beginning of the year. One Hindu New Year comes sometime in April or May.

The people in Morocco observe the beginning of the year on the tenth day of Muharram, the first month of the Islamic year. The Koreans celebrate their New Year during the first three days in January.

By the way, the custom of sending New Year's cards is a very old one. The Chinese have been doing it for more than one thousand years. Their cards carried the name of the visitor who came to call, but no greeting or message.

WHAT IS ESPERANTO?

Man for a long time has been trying to create a universal language that would serve all men all over the world as a common means of communication.

Since the seventeenth century, more than seven hundred such languages have been constructed. There are two kinds of such languages. The "a priori" kind have no connection with any existing language. The "a posteriori" kind use a mixture of existing languages. The most popular of the constructed languages is Esperanto.

It was invented by Ludwik Zamenhof, who lived in the town of Bialystok, Poland. As a young man, he saw that there was a great deal of enmity between the four groups of people who lived there—the Russians, Poles, Germans, and Jews. He felt that a common language would help these people get along better. When he was still in school, he had already worked out the beginnings of his international language.

In 1887, he published a brochure describing his language, and he used the pen name of Dr. Esperanto (one who hopes). Soon people in various parts of the world became interested in this language, which came to be called "Esperanto."

Today, Esperanto is spoken by about eight million people throughout the world. Even governments and international organizations recognize it in many ways. For example, you can send an international telegram in Esperanto. It is often used on radio broadcasts from official government stations.

There are many rules of grammar for this language, and here are a few. The definite article is "la" and does not change. All nouns end in "o," all adjectives in "a," all adverbs in "e," and all infinitives in "i." The plural of nouns and adjectives is formed by adding "j."

Here is the beginning of the Lord's Prayer in Esperanto: "Patro nia, kiu estas en la cielo, snkta estu via nomo; venu regeco via; esto volo via, kiel en la cielo, tiel ankau sur la tero."

WHAT IS THE DIFFERENCE BETWEEN A COLLEGE AND A UNIVERSITY?

Someday you may be preparing to enter a college or a university, and then you will become very interested in what each place has to offer and why you should try to go to one rather than another.

The chief difference between a college and a university is that the university usually includes a number of colleges. Many institutions pretend to be universities when they are not. On the other hand, some colleges are more like universities.

Here is one definition of a university given by the National Education Association: "an institution of higher education, having as a nucleus a college in which the so-called liberal arts are taught in a course of three or four years for a degree . . . and in addition one or more departments for the learned professions, medicine, law, or divinity."

The term "college" originally meant any society or union of persons engaged in common activity or granted certain powers and rights to carry on a common work. That's why the cardinals who elect the Pope at Rome are called the "College of Cardinals." And the United States has an "electoral college" that chooses the President and Vice-President. But in the United States, when we say college, we usually mean an institution attended after graduation from high school, and one that gives general, rather than highly specialized or technical training.

There are many "colleges" in the United States, however, that really should not be considered colleges. For example, any institution of higher education that has but one faculty (teachers in only one field of knowledge) and offers a single course of study is likely to be known as a college.

A college and a university differ in that the university includes several special colleges or schools. These special schools give instruction in professions such as law, medicine, forestry, and so on. Sometimes students go to college first, and then take graduate work at a university.

WHAT IS DONE WITH OLD MONEY?

Most of us would say: "If they don't know what to do with it, let them send it to me!" But the Government does know what to do with it. In fact, if old money weren't taken out of circulation at a regular rate, we'd find it a big nuisance, for torn and wrinkled paper money is inconvenient to handle.

The average life of a paper bill is only about a year, and for a dollar bill it's even less! So every day, the Treasury receives from banks and other sources worn and dirty bills to replace. How much? From four to five tons of paper money a day!

The old money is cancelled; that is, taken out of circulation. Then the bills are destroyed in a machine called a macerator, which does away with a million dollars a minute.

If you have damaged paper money, this doesn't make it worthless. If three-fifths of the note is preserved, you can send it to the Treasury

59

and redeem it at full value. If more than two-fifths but less than three-fifths is sent in, you will get half of its value.

The paper on which the notes are printed is specially made for the Government. It has in it a mixture of linen and cotton. In the paper are embedded colored fibers of silk, nylon, or other synthetic material. When you hold a bill up to the light, you can see some of these fibers.

United States money used to be of various sizes. From 1861 to 1928 it was 7 and 7/16 inches by 3 and 1/8 inches. But in 1928 it was made smaller, and the new size is what we have today—6 and 5/16 inches by 2 and 11/16 inches.

All United States money is coined or printed by the Treasury Department. Paper money is printed by the Bureau of Engraving and Printing at Washington.

WHY DID RUSSIA SELL ALASKA?

Today Alaska is our forty-ninth state. But at one time the tremendous potential and importance of this area were recognized by very few people. In fact, when it was bought by the United States in 1867 for $7,200,000 from Russia, it was called Seward's Folly.

William Seward was Secretary of State under Lincoln, and he had urged that we buy it. We obtained an area about twice the size of Texas, 586,400 square miles, at a price a little less than two cents an acre! Most Americans at the time thought it was too much to pay for such a barren, far-off place.

Alaska was one of the last areas of the world to be discovered and explored by white men. In the early eighteenth century, under Peter the Great, Russia extended its empire through Siberia and into the Pacific. In 1741, Vitus Bering, a Dane in the service of the Russian Navy, led an expedition of two small ships (his second expedition) that finally succeeded in reaching Alaska.

Throughout the rest of the eighteenth and much of the nineteenth century, Russia explored its Alaskan territory, then known as Russian America. It governed Alaska through the Russian America Company. But during this time also, sea captains of Spain, France, and Great

Britain explored the Alaska coast. The first United States vessels reached Alaska in 1788.

In 1821 Russia declared other nations were not to be allowed to trade or fish or do business north of a certain line. But in 1824 and 1825 Russia signed treaties with England and the United States giving them trading rights.

When the Crimean War broke out in 1854, the Russians felt that they had too much trouble at home to bother with Alaska. They also felt that Alaska was too exposed and too far away for Russia to be able to protect it. Negotiations were started in 1859 to sell Alaska to the United States. The Civil War temporarily halted negotiations, but in 1867 the sale was made.

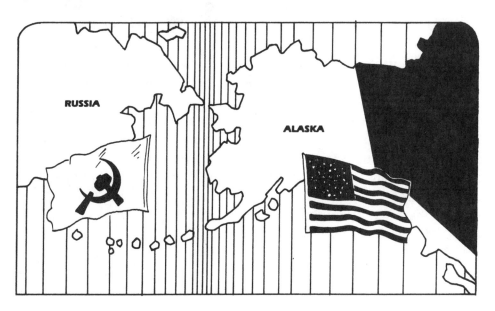

CHAPTER 2
HOW THINGS BEGAN

WHERE WERE THE FIRST FOSSILS FOUND?

During the past two to three billion years, many forms of life, both plant and animal, have inhabited the earth and then become extinct. We know about them through the study of fossils.

Most fossils are the remains of plants and animals preserved in rock. Fossils take many forms. Sometimes they are shells, bones, scales, or other hard parts of animals; more often, chemicals replace the hard parts. The tracks of animals are also fossils.

Fossils had existed for millions of years before man began to read their story of past life on earth. Yet there is evidence that some early men had seen fossils and recognized them as something special. A necklace of fossil sea shells was found with the skeleton of a woman who died thirty thousand years ago.

The scholars of ancient Greece and Rome found fossil sea shells far up in the mountains. They realized that these shells were the remains of animals that had once lived in the sea. And so they reasoned that in past ages these mountains had been under the sea.

Scientists did not really begin to study fossils until the late 1700's. One of the first men to do so was Baron Georges Cuvier, a great French naturalist. In the rocks along the river banks near Paris, Cuvier found the bones of elephants, hippopotamuses, and many other animals no longer seen in that region. He realized that the climate around

Paris must once have been very different, something like the climate of India and Africa today.

Then an Englishman named William Smith began to study fossils all over England. He discovered that each kind of rock had its own group of fossils. Older rocks would generally contain simpler fossils than newer rocks. From this he was able to tell the relative age of the rocks. Charles Darwin later used evidence from fossils to show how living forms developed from past forms, and how higher forms might have developed from simpler ones.

WHEN DID CIVILIZATION BEGIN?

It took man a long, long time to reach what we call a state of civilization. At first he lived in a state of savagery, much like animals. He had no language, and obtained food wherever he could find it.

Later on he had a family organization, learned to make fire, and still later, how to make tools and hunt for food. He invented pottery so that he could cook his food, began to live in tribes, and was able to move to new places.

The next stage of man, which is called barbarism, saw him learn how to raise food from seeds and how to tame animals. Then he began to smelt metals, such as copper and iron, so that he could make better weapons. He also began to build houses. When he invented a system of picture writing, it marked the end of barbarism and the beginning of civilization.

The invention of writing is considered the beginning of civilization, because it enabled man to keep records of past happenings. In this way, people could learn from the experience of others. This happened about five thousand or six thousand years ago.

By the time man reached this stage, he had developed in other ways, too. He had built up agriculture and industry to the point where people could live in villages and even in cities. There was government, there was trade, there were laws, and there were migrations of people.

The earliest civilizations that are known to us in history are those of the Egyptians and the Babylonians. The Egyptians had a form of writing four thousand five hundred years ago. They had a system of government and an understanding of mathematics (used in building the pyramids); they had a calendar, employed architects, and knew how to use various machines.

There was also a civilization on the island of Crete about four thousand years ago; and the Sumerian people, who lived along the Tigris and Euphrates rivers, had a civilization as far back as four thousand five hundred years ago.

DID PEOPLE ALWAYS LIVE IN FAMILIES?

No one knows how the first family started. Excavations in ancient caves show that men, women, and children lived together in small groups. It is not certain that the groups separated at first into units of father, mother, and children that we think of as a family, although the women probably cared for their own children. The "family" kept warm with fire and protected themselves against wild animals with simple weapons.

A family kind of life is more necessary among human beings than among other creatures. This is because the most helpless creature on earth is the human baby. Most insects and other members of the lower forms of life can move about and get their own food as soon as they are hatched. But the young of the higher forms of life—human infants, baby bears, and other animals—must be fed and protected.

The father (human or animal) usually brings the food for the mother and protects the young against enemies. The mother is most important, for she provides the milk for the baby. Thus the family is formed because it is necessary for the young and adults to stay together.

During the hundreds of thousands of years that family life has existed, different forms of family organization have developed among different peoples. In some tribes, the mother's brother was head of the family. The father had little to do with the children.

The pharaohs in ancient Egypt married their sisters. During Biblical times and earlier, a man might have two or more wives. Among some peoples a woman might have several husbands. The marriage of a man or woman to more than one mate is called polygamy.

There are still families in Africa and the Near East with more than one wife, but the practice seems to be dying out.

HOW DID ANIMALS GET THEIR NAMES?

Not all the English names of animals came about the same way. Some are just the English word for a name that already existed in another language. Others are combinations of words that describe the animal. Let's consider the names of some animals and see how they originated.

Hippopotamus is the Greek for river horse. *Hippos* meant horse, and *potamos* meant river. Rhinoceros is a Latin term derived from two Greek words. *Rinos* meant the "nose," and *keras* was a "horn." And the rhinoceros has a horn on its nose!

Leopard comes from the Latin *leopardus,* which meant a spotted lion. Lion comes from the Latin *leon.* Camel comes from the Arabic *gamel,* which was *camelos* in Latin.

Wolf is a modern spelling of the Anglo-Saxon *wulf,* which goes back to the Latin *vulpes,* and which meant fox. Our name fox comes from the Icelandic *fax,* which meant a hair-mane. The name opossum comes from *opassum,* which is what the Indians of Virginia called this animal.

Bull comes from the Anglo-Saxon *belkan,* which meant to roar. Deer was originally *deor* in Anglo-Saxon, and meant a wild animal. Porcupine comes from two Latin words: *porcus,* a swine, and *spina,* a thorn. So it's a pig with thorns.

When we call a cat a puss it goes back to the Egyptians. They called a cat *pasht,* which meant the moon, because cats were active at night. This became shortened to *pas,* and that's how we got puss.

The name poodle comes from the German *pudel,* which meant a puddle. This was because it was a water dog. And the word dog itself is a contraction of the Icelandic *doggr.* These are only a few names of animals, but you can see how they originated in many different ways.

WHO BUILT THE FIRST CASTLE?

The idea of a castle is connected with defense. In fact, the word "castle" comes from a Latin word meaning *fort.* So a castle was a home of a ruler or lord that could be defended.

Even in ancient Egypt, the royal palaces were fortified with towers and parapets, and so were like castles. In ancient Greece, too, the chieftains fortified their palaces. But the castle as we think of it really came into its own during the Middle Ages in western Europe, from A.D. 1000 to A.D. 1500.

The reason for this was the feudal system. Individual nobles controlled their own sections of the country and their people. They would often attack or take advantage of neighboring areas in order to strengthen their power. And, of course, they would be attacked in return. So they had to make their own homes into strong forts, and thus built what we call castles.

Since the conditions were pretty much alike in most of Europe, the castles that were built were quite similar, whether they were in France, Germany, Spain, or England. One of the first such structures was the Tower of London, begun in 1078 by William the Conqueror. It was several stories high, had double walls, small windows, and spiral staircases in the corners of the tower. The lord and his garrison of troops lived there.

Another early castle, Hedingham Castle, in Essex, England, was built in 1130. It had double walls of stone twenty feet thick, and its corners were even thicker. There was a great center hall, two stories high. The only light came from a few small windows high up in the wall. It was planned this way for reasons of defense; few and small windows were good protection.

Later on, castles were built around inner courtyards, so that there would be more room for the people living in them, and more comfortable facilities could be set up.

WHO INVENTED THE FIRST PLOW?

Before a farmer can plant his seeds, he must prepare the ground by plowing. The plow breaks up the hard ground and turns the soil over.

The plow is a very ancient invention, and no one knows who made the first plow. The earliest plows that have been found are about five thousand years old. The main purpose of all plows is to stir up the soil by dragging or raking something through it. At first the plow was just a forked stick or log, pulled by men or women. Later, men learned to use animals to pull plows.

Gradually the shape of the plowing stick was changed so that it would work better. The bottom of the stick was shaped into a pointed blade called the plowshare. This helped the plow cut through the ground more easily.

Then curved sides were added to the plow. These sides turn the soil over as it is plowed up and break it up more thoroughly. The sides are called moldboards. Together the plowshare and moldboards are called the plow bottom. The type of plow that is most commonly used today is called a moldboard plow.

The plowshare was made much stronger and sharper by cutting it out of metal. In the eighteenth century the British began making cast-iron plowshares. In 1797 Charles Newbold, an American inventor, patented the first American cast-iron plow. Modern plows are made of cast iron or steel, depending on what kind of soil the plow is to be used in.

Did you know that Thomas Jefferson used mathematics to find the best shape for a plow bottom (the plowshare plus the moldboards) and helped make the cast-iron plow popular?

In dry, hard soils, disk plows are used instead of moldboard plows. Instead of pointed blades on the bottom, disk plows have sharp-edged steel disks. Disk plows are good for rocky soil because they can roll over rocks that might stop or damage a moldboard plow. Disk plows are also very good for plowing old plants into the soil to enrich it.

WHERE DID CORN ORIGINATE?

Corn, or maize, is one of the most useful plants known to man. Today it is an important crop in southern Europe, Africa, parts of Asia, and, of course, the United States.

Scientists believe that it originated somewhere in Central or South America. Prehistoric Indians probably selected seeds year after year from wild grasses. After several centuries they had developed a plant very much like the corn we know today. Corn is a plant that cannot survive unless man cares for it. No wild plants closely resembling corn are now known.

Indians had their own stories about the origin of corn. In one tale a young girl turned herself into a corn plant to give mankind a new grain. She left her hair on the plant as corn silks to remind people to take good care of her gift.

The Indians liked corn with blue, red, and black kernels. They gave their colorful corn to the Pilgrims to feed them during the first cold winter in America. The next year the Pilgrims shared their own harvest with the Indians. This was the first Thanksgiving.

Corn was first introduced to the Old World as maize by Christopher Columbus. Maize was the Indian name for the grain. It has kept this name, spelled in a variety of ways, in most countries. Since the word "corn" in England meant any kind of grain, the Pilgrims called this new grain "Indian corn."

Today there are six chief types of corn. Dent corn is the most widely grown. It has a notch at the top of the kernel. Flint corn has hard kernels and withstands cold and disease.

The corn we eat is usually sweet corn, flour corn, or popcorn. Sweet corn is high in sugar. Flour corn is used to make flour. Popcorn is corn that bursts from its small, hard-shelled kernels when heated.

WHERE DID ORANGES ORIGINATE?

There are records that show that in China the orange was known at least four thousand years ago!

There are two kinds of orange tree, the sweet and the sour. The sour orange was the first orange grown in Europe. It was introduced by the Moors who invaded southern Spain and Sicily around the ninth century.

By the eleventh century the Moors were quite strongly in control of the conquered countries, and they planted sour orange and other trees. Sour oranges were widely grown in southern Europe until the fifteenth century, when increased trade with the Orient brought sweet oranges to Europe. Although some sour oranges are still grown and eaten, they are now used mainly as rootstocks for sweet oranges.

Sweet oranges were at first a luxury that only very rich people could afford. Kings and nobles paid great prices to obtain orange trees, which they planted in their gardens.

In the colder countries the delicate trees would be killed during a cold winter, so special greenhouses, called orangeries, were built. The orange trees were planted in tubs. During the summer they were moved outside, but in winter they were kept safe behind glass in the orangeries, where they could bloom despite the cold outside.

Did you know that when Christopher Columbus sailed for the New World he carried seeds of oranges and many other citrus fruits with him? The seeds were planted on the island of Hispaniola. Citrus trees flourished in the tropical climate of the West Indies and what is now Florida.

The Indians ate the oranges and, as they traveled about, they dropped the seeds. Planted in this way, groves of citrus trees were soon growing wild.

Today the United States leads the world in the production of oranges. The state of Florida has the greatest number of orange trees and produces more sweet oranges than any other state—or country!

WHERE DID WATERMELONS ORIGINATE?

On a hot summer day is there anything that tastes as good as a cold, juicy watermelon? It's no wonder then that this fruit has been enjoyed by man for thousands of years.

The watermelon originated in tropical Africa and spread from there to every possible place where the soil and climate were right. In ancient Sanskrit there is a word for watermelon, and there are early Egyptian drawings that show watermelons. So we know that it has been cultivated for more than four thousand years!

The watermelon is one of several types of melons, all of which belong to the gourd family. Like cucumbers, they are trailing annual vines with flat, lobed leaves and bell-shaped flowers.

Muskmelons are another ancient type of melon, which grew originally in southern Asia. All muskmelons have a faint, musky perfume, which gives them their name. Muskmelons are often called cantaloupes.

The Casaba and the honeydew melons ripen late in the season and keep better than other melons. Casaba melons are large, with smooth, yellowish-green rinds. Their flavor is delicate and their flesh is pale green. Honeydew melons have an even smoother rind, and their flesh is deeper green than that of Casaba melons.

Watermelons are considerably larger than muskmelons, and much juicier. Some watermelons weigh more than fifty pounds, but most of them are smaller. The rind is hard and green, often mottled or striped with lighter green. The flesh is pinkish, yellowish, or red.

Watermelons need a long growing season and a hot climate. They are planted after the ground is warm and there is no danger of frost. Watermelons are usually eaten fresh, but they can be pickled and the rind made into a preserve. In Oriental countries their seeds are considered a delicacy.

WHEN WAS WINE FIRST MADE?

Wine is the fermented juice of grapes. It has been enjoyed by man for thousands of years.

Probably the first people to make wine were Persian farmers living near the Caspian Sea. The Egyptians learned how to make wine from them as long ago as 3000 B.C. Pictures on the walls of tombs in the pyramids show the ancient Egyptians making wine.

Wine was common in the everyday life of the early Greeks and Romans. It was important to their religious ceremonies. The god of wine was called Bacchus by the Romans and Dionysus by the Greeks.

In the fourth century B.C., the Greek conqueror Alexander the Great carried grapevines and the knowledge of wine-making to Central Asia. The Greeks also took vines to southern France. Roman invaders probably took vines to northern France and Germany in later centuries.

When Leif Ericson landed on the eastern coast of North America in about 1000 A.D. he found so many wild grapevines growing there that he called the place Vinland. Later, Spanish explorers and missionaries brought grapevines from Europe to California.

Wine was used ceremonially in many ancient religions. And it is used today in many Christian and Jewish religious ceremonies. In times when pure water was scarce, wine was considered safe and healthful to drink.

Wine can be made from many fruits and plants that contain natural sugar. But most wine is made from grapes. When we say "wine," without using a descriptive name, such as "peach wine" or "blackberry wine," we always mean grape wine.

There are more than eight thousand varieties of grapes that can be used to make wine.

WHO MADE THE FIRST TABLE?

Can you imagine a house without a table in it? A table fills so many needs—eating, writing, playing games, holding lamps, and so on—that tables seem to have existed since the beginning of civilization.

A small table, made of metal or wood, was known to the Sumerians, and theirs is the first civilization of which we have any records. The Babylonians and Assyrians got the idea from them, as did the Egyptians. The Egyptians produced small, low tables that were beautifully designed and had fine workmanship.

The Greeks, who adapted many things from the Egyptian civilization, developed all kinds of furniture, including tables. Their tables were made of marble, metals, and inlaid woods.

Then the Romans carried the development of furniture to an even higher level. They not only had tables made entirely of metal or wood, but they also made costly ornamental tables that were delicately carved and inlaid with ivory and precious metals. The legs were carved into sphinxes, fluted columns, or to resemble the legs of rams or lions.

It was the custom among them to recline rather than sit at the dining table, so the tables were low in height. By the way, in ancient times, tables of any kind were owned only by the rich.

During the Middle Ages, tables appeared in all kinds of shapes: circular, oval, and oblong. But they were made quite simply—just boards supported by a fixed or folding trestle. They were covered with tablecloths that reached to the floor in order to hide the supports. After a meal, they were cleared out of the way.

During the sixteenth century, in the castles of the rich, there would be a fixed table in the great hall. This was reserved for the nobility, and ordinary people sat at smaller, separate tables or boards.

WHY DO MEN RAISE THEIR HATS TO LADIES?

This custom, like so many others that we practice today, passed through many stages of development before it came down to us.

Long, long ago, uncovering one's body in the presence of another person was considered a sign of respect and deference. Usually, it was

the upper part of the body that was uncovered. In time, instead of uncovering the body, it was considered enough to uncover one's head. And gradually, the mere raising of the hat was all that was necessary to show respect.

During the age of knights, it was the custom for a knight to wear his full armor in public. But when a knight came among friends, he would remove his helmet. This was a symbol of the fact that he felt safe among friends and didn't need the protection of his helmet.

This custom, combined with the already existing custom of uncovering one's head as a sign of respect, created the tradition of raising the hat as a mark of courtesy. In our civilization, of course, it is men who are expected to show signs of courtesy to women, so the custom of raising the hat is still practiced by men today!

WHEN DID PEOPLE FIRST FREEZE FOOD?

We think of frozen food as a new invention, but it is actually one of the oldest methods known for preserving food. From the days when man first inhabited cold regions, he froze fish, game, and other meats for future use.

The first known patent for freezing food was granted as early as 1852 in England. The method used was to immerse the food in an ice-

and-salt brine. Many other patents were granted for freezing food at that time, all using ice-and-salt mixtures.

But frozen foods could not be used extensively until the development of mechanical refrigeration. This made it possible to freeze and transport meats over long distances.

Early in the twentieth century, attempts were made to preserve foods other than meats and fish by freezing. A man called H. S. Baker froze fruits in Colorado as early as 1908. The purpose of this was to freeze the part of the fruit crop that couldn't be marketed and sell it for use later.

Only certain fruits were frozen at first, chiefly strawberries and cherries. They were frozen by what is known as the cold-pack method. This means placing barrels or containers of the fruit in large storage rooms where the temperature is maintained at 10 and 15 degrees below zero fahrenheit.

In 1916, experiments in Germany showed that foods could be frozen by the quick-freeze method, which meant freezing the food in a few hours instead of in several days. In 1917 a man called Clarence Birdseye began to work on methods for freezing food in small containers for sale in stores. It wasn't until 1919 that the first commercial pack of this type was put on the market.

As the result of his experiments and the work of others, it was found that many vegetables could also be preserved in this manner, and the frozen-food industry was on its way.

WHEN WAS COAL FIRST USED?

Coal has been used by man since very ancient times. Probably the first people to use it were the Chinese. There are records to show the Chinese used coal to smelt copper and iron perhaps as far back in time as three thousand years ago.

Coal is mentioned in the Bible. In the Book of Proverbs we read: "As coals are to burning coals, and wood to fire, so is a contentious man to kindle strife." The Greek philosopher Aristotle, who lived from 384 to 322 B.C., mentions coal in his writings.

During the period when the Romans occupied Britain, which began about 50 B.C., coal was used. We know this because in the ruins of Roman villas in Britain both coal and cinders have been found.

Here is an interesting fact about a certain coal mine. There are records that show that coal was mined in the Dutch province of Limburg in the year 1113. This mine, now known as the Domaniale Mine, is still being used and produces the most coal in the Netherlands!

During the mid-thirteenth century, women and children gathered what was known as sea coal along the English coast, and there were already several mines in England. Blacksmiths needed the coal for heating the iron for their smithies. Owners of small shops kept their places warm with coal. And poor people preferred coal to wood for heating purposes because it was cheaper.

By the way, the nobility at that time refused to have anything to do with coal. They wouldn't enter a house in which coal was burned or eat food that had been cooked over coal fires. They believed the smoke poisoned the food. And, of course, since houses at that time didn't have chimneys, smoke used to fill the rooms, which is what made people suspicious of coal.

After the invention of the steam engine, which made it possible to transport coal from the mines, the use of coal finally became common.

WHEN WAS METAL FIRST USED?

About six thousand years ago man lived in what we call the Stone Age. This is because he made most of his tools and weapons out of stone. He had not yet learned how to use metals.

Probably the first metals man learned how to use were copper and gold. The reason is that these metals occur in nature in a free state as well as in ores. Man found nuggets of copper and gold and was able to hammer them into various shapes without having to melt them. We don't know the date when man discovered how to use these metals, but we do know that copper was used as long ago as 5000 B.C. Gold was first used some time before 4000 B.C.

By about 3000 B.C., man had learned some of the most important things about using metals. By this time the metals silver and lead had been discovered, too, but copper was the one used most since it was the strongest and most plentiful.

Man first learned to beat metal into useful shapes, such as bowls, tools, and weapons. Once he began using metals, he discovered the processes of annealing (making a metal soft and tough by heating and then slowly cooling it), melting, casting, and smelting. Also, he could get copper from its ore, which was more plentiful than the nuggets.

Later man discovered tin and learned to mix copper and tin, which made bronze. From about 3500 B.C. to about 1200 B.C., bronze was the most important material for making tools and weapons. This period is called the Bronze Age.

Man knew about iron from meteorites he found, long before he discovered how to smelt it from its ore. By about 1200 B.C., man had learned how to work iron, and this knowledge spread all over the world. Iron replaced bronze for most uses. This was the beginning of the Iron Age.

By the time of the Romans, seven metals were known: gold, copper, silver, lead, tin, iron, and mercury.

WHO MADE THE FIRST TIMEPIECE?

When we talk of a timepiece, we mean an instrument to measure time. But man found ways of measuring time long before he invented any instruments to do so.

The rising and setting of the sun were man's first units of time. The lengthening and shortening of shadows made by sticks, stones,

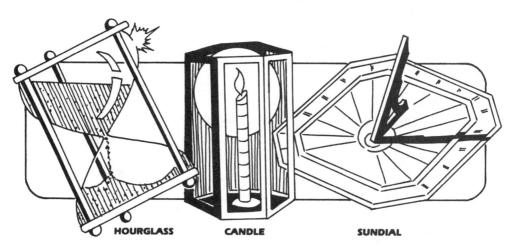

HOURGLASS   CANDLE   SUNDIAL

and trees also gave him an idea of the general time of the day. And the movements of the stars furnished him with a kind of gigantic clock. Man noticed that as the night passed, different stars became visible.

The ancient Egyptians divided the night into twelve time periods, corresponding to the rising of twelve stars. They divided the day into twelve periods also, and our twenty-four-hour day is based on the Egyptian division of day and night. The Egyptians also made shadow clocks—blocks of wood with pointers. Eventually these shadow clocks, or sundials, had twelve periods of time to divide the day—so they were the first timepieces.

The next kind of timepiece developed by man used fire and water. A candle with notches cut in the side will measure time as it burns from notch to notch. A dish with a small hole in the bottom can be set on water. After a certain period of time the floating dish will fill with water and sink.

About two thousand years ago, man developed still another kind of timepiece—the hourglass. This consisted of two hollow glass containers connected so that sand could flow from one to the other. The top container was filled with enough sand to flow through the hole for one hour.

About 140 B.C.the Greeks and Romans used the toothed wheel to improve the water clock. A float placed in a container rose as water trickled into the container. The float was connected to a toothed wheel. The wheel turned a pointer that gradually moved from one hour-mark to another.

The first true mechanical clock was invented about fourteen hundred years later. A weight was attached to a cord wound on a spool. As the cord unwound, it turned the spool, which moved a series of toothed wheels, or gears. The wheels turned a hand on a dial.

WHEN WAS THE WASHING MACHINE INVENTED?

Everybody knows about washing machines, but in many homes they are still a luxury. Before any kind of mechanical washers were invented, home washing was done in a wooden or galvanized tub. The wash was rubbed on a corrugated washboard to force the water through and the dirt out. Then the wash was put through a wringer to squeeze out the excess water, and finally it was hung out on a line to dry.

One of the first home washing machines was made in 1858 by Hamilton Smith of Pittsburgh, Pennsylvania. This home washer was operated by turning a crank at the side that rotated paddles that were inside the tub. There was another early washing machine that imitated the scrubbing action of a washboard.

But these first machines were not successful. The clothes often became tangled, knotted, or torn. It wasn't until 1907 that a practical washing machine was developed that operated by motor. By 1912 nearly all makers of home washing machines were making them to be driven by electric power.

The tubs of the first washing machines were made of wood. Gradually, the manufacturers turned to metal: copper, galvanized steel, aluminum, and zinc. By 1961 practically all tubs were made of porcelain enamel, because such machines could resist the strong washing powders and all temperatures of water.

The agitator was developed in 1922. Most agitators consist of a cone with several fins at its lower end. The agitator moves the wash up and down and side to side. The fully automatic washing machine first appeared in 1937.

Most washing machines hold between eight and ten pounds of wash. They generally use between thirty-five and forty-five gallons of water per wash, and the water temperature is usually kept between 135 and 165 degrees fahrenheit.

The first successful home dryer was built in 1930. A combination washer-dryer was first put on the market in 1953.

WHEN WERE WHEELS INVENTED?

The wheel was one of man's greatest inventions. Before men had wheels, they moved heavy loads on sleds pulled by men or oxen.

The earliest known wheels were made in ancient Mesopotamia (modern Iraq) between 3500 and 3000 B.C. They were of two kinds: the cart wheel and the potter's wheel. The potter's wheel was the ancestor of our pulleys, water wheels, gear wheels, clockwork, and other wheeled machinery.

The first carts were simply sleds mounted on wheels. The idea of mounting a sled on wheels probably came from the practice of putting logs under a sled to act as rollers. As the sled rolled forward, the rollers were picked up behind it and laid down again in front of the sled.

The earliest wheels were probably fastened solidly to their axles. Wheel and axle turned together. When a cart with wheels of this kind rounded a corner, the outer wheel traveled farther than the inner wheel. So one wheel or the other had to skid or drag.

A later invention—fastening the axle to the vehicle and letting the wheels spin freely—made turning much easier.

The first wheeled vehicles were farm carts, war chariots, royal hearses, and the sacred wagons of the gods.

Early carts and chariots were made with two wheels or with four. But the early four-wheeled vehicles were not practical. Both the front and rear axles were fastened to the body. Since neither axle could swing, the vehicle could not make sharp turns. About two thousand years ago someone developed a front axle that was pivotal so it could turn right and left.

The spoked wheel was invented in southwestern Asia about 2000 B.C.

WHAT WAS THE SANTA FE TRAIL?

The Santa Fe Trail was a traders' path. It was never an actual road, but rather a broad route that followed rivers and wagon ruts. It led from the Missouri River to Santa Fe, New Mexico.

The people of Santa Fe, which was a Mexican mission town, wanted to trade with Americans, but Mexico's rulers forbade this. When Mexico rebelled against Spain in 1820, Santa Fe was opened to American trade.

The first man to reach Mexico after trade was opened was William Becknell, who is called the "Father of the Sante Fe Trail." On his return trip, snow clogged the northern trail he had planned to follow, so he took a shortcut across the Cimarron Desert. This Cimarron Cutoff became part of the Santa Fe Trail.

When Becknell returned to his home in Franklin, Missouri in January, 1822, he poured out the Mexican silver dollars he had received for his goods onto the sidewalk, to the amazement of his neighbors. People became interested in carrying on such profitable trade, so Becknell organized a trading party. They planned to take wagons where wagons had never gone before.

Becknell and his party crossed the Missouri, struck out across the Great Plains to the Arkansas River, and followed its course. Often they had to float or drag wagons across the river to avoid steep cliffs. Going through the Cimarron Cutoff meant crossing fifty miles of dry, hot wasteland without a landmark to help them find their way.

Finally they reached the Cimarron River and crossed it. They were safely past the desert. Over three hundred miles of rough travel through foothills brought them to Sante Fe. They had proved men could take wagons over the Trail.

When they returned and showed their rich profits, others flocked to the trade. From 1822 to 1843, caravans headed west each spring over the Sante Fe Trail. Trouble with Mexico stopped the trade in 1843, but after the Mexican War ended, Sante Fe was in American territory. The Trail became one of the roads serving California gold hunters.

WHY WERE COVERED BRIDGES BUILT?

There are not many covered bridges left in America today, and those that still stand have become tourist attractions. This is not only because they are rare, but many are quite beautiful and quaint.

At one time, covered bridges dotted the American countryside from the Atlantic coast to the Ohio River. The bridges looked like square tunnels with peaked roofs. Why were these bridges built with covers?

Some people claim that the bridges were covered so that horses would not be frightened by the water underneath. Others say that they were built as a shelter for travelers in bad weather.

Actually the coverings were designed to protect the wooden framework and flooring of the bridges and keep them from rotting. Some of these covered bridges still standing today are more than one hundred years old!

Many of these bridges have been destroyed to make room for modern highways. To protect the bridges that are left, the National Society for the Preservation of Covered Bridges has been established. Many states also try to protect the bridges by making them historical landmarks.

When it comes to unusual bridges, two of the most interesting are London Bridge and the Ponte Vecchio in Florence, Italy. London Bridge was the first one over the Thames River to be built entirely of masonry. Houses were gradually erected on the bridge until it was covered with buildings. The old London Bridge was replaced by the new London Bridge about 1830.

The Ponte Vecchio was another bridge on which people lived. It was built in 1345, and is still lined with houses. Most of these houses are now used for shops.

WHO MADE THE FIRST BOAT?

If you lived near a body of water and had never seen or heard of a boat before, what would you do? You'd probably want to get across the water or move down it in some way, and you'd look for something that would hold you up on the water.

In very much this way, primitive man probably discovered that if he tied some brush or tree trunks together, and if he used a stick or a branch as a pole or paddle, he could get across a river or lake. And thus the idea of a boat was born.

This kind of boat, consisting of objects that float being tied together, was really a raft. But the problem with a raft is that it doesn't move very fast, and water washes over it and through it.

So in looking for some kind of faster and drier boat, primitive man thought of hollowing out a tree trunk. It was faster and fairly watertight. But you couldn't carry as much in this kind of boat as on a raft, and it could easily tip over.

So primitive man tried to improve the "dug-out" kind of boat. He shaped the bow and stern for greater speed; he bulged out the sides for more stability; he flattened out the bottom. Then he invented the keel, and he tried to raise the sides by building them up with planks.

Meanwhile, those who were still using the raft began to make improvements on it, too. They put a floor on the raft composed of timbers that were squared and shaped. They built a platform on it for greater comfort and protection (which was the beginning of the deck). They built up the sides and turned up the ends. And they had a kind of boat that later on was to become an ark, or punt, or junk—all types of flat-bottomed boats.

In time, the raft and the dug-out boats began to have many features in common. From then on it was a question of combining the best features of each, depending on what kind of boat was needed. So we can say that boats as we know them today began with both these ideas first thought of by primitive man.

WHO WERE THE FIRST PEOPLE TO USE SAILS?

A long, long time ago man made an important discovery, though nobody knows exactly when it happened. The discovery was that it was easy to move a boat along in the same direction as the wind.

All that was needed was to hoist up a section of skins, cloth, or something like it on a stick. With such a crude sail the boat would move along easily and it wouldn't be necessary to row it.

Of course, a real sailing vessel has another advantage: it can also sail against the wind. For this, it is necessary to know how to tack, or to approach by zigzags. It was a long time before ships and sails and this kind of know-how were developed.

On the way to this kind of use of sails, there were many steps. The ancient Egyptians had ships that used both oars and huge sails. At first, their ships were used only on the Nile River, but later they went out to sea. But the sails were only used with a following wind.

The Greeks and Romans developed a kind of ship called a galley. It used slaves to do the rowing, and it also had a sail that was used only with a following wind.

Another kind of ship they developed, called "round" ships, were used to carry cargoes. At first, these ships had only one mast with one great sail. But around the time of Christ these ships already had an additional small mast and sail in the bow, and sometimes also a small topsail.

These ships were still not able to head into the wind, but some of them could operate with the wind coming in on the side.

The Vikings also developed ships with sails, and by 800 A.D. had ships with large square sails.

WHAT WERE THE FIRST OCEAN LINERS?

Today most travel across oceans is done by air, though ocean liners are still in use. Ocean-liner service across the Atlantic started in 1816. The first line to run ships on a regular schedule was the Black Ball Line of New York. Its ships sailed between New York and Liverpool, England. Soon afterward other ship lines began operating.

The early liners were sailing ships. They were called packet ships because they carried packets of mail as well as passengers. The ships were not very comfortable. First-class passengers had only small cabins. Travelers in the cheapest class, called the steerage, had no cabins at all. They slept on bunks of rough boards, stacked three deep in low, narrow spaces below decks.

On some ship lines the steerage passengers had to bring their own food. Each passenger had to show his supply of food before he was allowed aboard. The required supply included quantities of biscuits, flour, potatoes, tea, sugar, molasses, two hams, a tin pot, frying pan, mug, teapot, knife, fork and spoon. To help provide milk and food for other passengers, most packet ships had a cow and a flock of chickens on board!

The first steam-powered ship to cross the Atlantic was the American vessel *Savannah*. In 1819 she made the trip from Savannah, Georgia, to Liverpool in twenty-nine days. The *Savannah* used her sails most of the way, running on steam power only when the winds died down.

Sails were carried on the early steamships because seamen didn't trust the new steam power. They were afraid that the steam engine might break down in mid-ocean or that the fuel might run out.

One of the famous early steamships had paddle wheels and screw propellers. This was the *Great Eastern*. She was 692 feet long and 83 feet wide, and remained the world's largest ship for forty years.

HOW DID NAVIES ORIGINATE?

Did you know that originally the navy of a country meant all of its ships, whether used for war, the carrying of merchandise, or fishing? Today, of course, the word "navy" has come to mean a country's fighting ships and those that help in warfare.

The first navies were created when the armed men of a tribe or town went to sea in the largest ships they had in order to give battle to their enemies or raid territory from the sea. The ships used were ordinary fishing or commercial ships. Only later on were ships especially designed for purposes of war.

At the time of the ancient Greeks and Romans, the very first long ships were built for speed in war, instead of round ones to carry merchandise. When the Persians threatened to attack Athens in 483 B.C., the Greeks increased their navy from fifty to one hundred long ships. By the end of the fifth century B.C. this fleet of long ships had increased to 300 and later even to 360, which makes it quite a navy! In times of peace these warships were kept on slips and under cover in sheds.

The most ancient warships were many-oared galleys, each requiring a great number of rowers. These great rowing galleys were used to ram other ships or as a means of boarding the enemy ships.

In both the ancient Greek and Roman navies there were many similarities to the organization of a modern navy. The Greeks had a captain, a sailing master, a number of petty officers, seamen and oarsmen, and soldiers or marines who did the fighting. The Romans always had a body of soldiers, called the *classici,* who were especially assigned to service in the navy.

Today, of course, a navy is a very complicated organization with dozens of types of ships and units organized to maintain them.

WHEN DID MEN BEGIN UNDERWATER EXPLORATION?

The first underwater explorer was probably looking for something to eat.

Hundreds of thousands of years ago, people knew how to get fish from the water. These early fishermen lived on the shores of lakes in Africa, and they probably waded in to make the catch with their hands.

Wading led to swimming. Then swimmers learned how to hold their breath and became divers. The first dives were along lakeshores and seacoasts where the water was deep and clear. Gradually divers learned to explore at greater and greater depths.

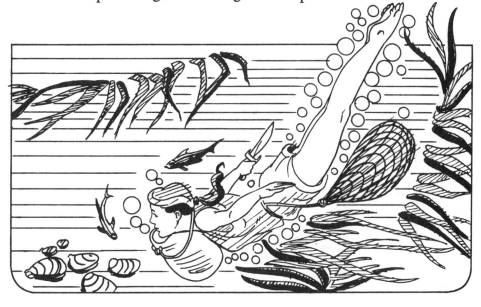

They found all sorts of interesting and useful things to bring back. There were shellfish to eat, and there were beautiful colored corals and shells that people used for beads or for money. As far back as four thousand years ago, Indians did deep diving off the coast of Peru to obtain mussels, a kind of shellfish, which was one of their favorite foods.

At the same time—thousands of years ago —on the other side of the world, men were bringing up oysters from the Arabian Gulf, but not to eat. These divers wanted the pearls that sometimes grew inside the shell in the soft part of the oyster's body. The pearls were made into jewelry, just as they are now.

The men of ancient Greece and Turkey are sometimes called the fathers of modern diving. They began exploring for sponges in the Aegean Sea more than two thousand years ago, and what they learned is still useful today.

They discovered that the more air they could take down with them, the longer they could stay underwater. One of them finally thought of carrying extra air down in a device called a water bladder.

This was made from the skin of a goat, sheep, or pig. It was oiled and made waterproof. All but one opening was sewn up tightly. The diver would blow the skin full of air, and with a heavy stone to keep himself underwater, would go down into the water. He could work for some time, getting air from the inflated skin as he needed it.

HOW DID SWIMMING START?

Man does not swim naturally, as certain animals do. He has had to learn how to swim.

Originally, man must have learned to swim by watching animals that swim by instinct. Early man probably had to learn how to swim in order to survive under certain conditions.

The first effort man made to swim imitated a dog. Such a stroke has always been known as the "dog paddle." But then man wanted to find a way of swimming that gave him more buoyancy and an opportunity to coordinate the motions of the arms and legs. So more than two thousand years ago he developed the method of swimming known as the breast stroke. This stroke is still used by many people for restful distance swimming in rough open water.

The next stroke that man developed in swimming was the side stroke. In this stroke the "scissors kick" was used. After that came the "over-arm" side stroke. In this, the upper arm was extended out of water. It allowed a longer arm pull and produced greater speed.

The next stroke to be developed is called the Trudgen, after John Trudgen, an Englishman who introduced it in 1783. This consists of an alternate over-arm stroke and a scissors kick. He broke so many records with this stroke that many people adopted it.

Next we come to the crawl stroke. It is called that because in its original form it resembled a man crawling. It was brought to England in 1902 by Richard Cavill, who had learned it in Australia, where the natives used it. It was first called the Australian crawl. People using the crawl stroke broke so many swimming records that it was adopted as the speediest of all strokes.

By the way, swimming was rated highly in the ancient days of Greece and Rome and was used as part of the training of warriors.

WHO WAS THE FIRST TO GO UP IN A BALLOON?

Why does a balloon go up? Air itself is made up of gases, the chief ones being oxygen and nitrogen. Certain other gases are lighter than air. One of these is helium, and that is why a balloon filled with helium rises. Hot air will also make a balloon rise, because it is lighter than cold air.

Man sent balloons up into the air before he went up with them. The first big balloon was built by two French brothers called Montgolfier. On June 5, 1783, they launched their balloon by building a fire under it. When hot air from the fire filled the balloon, the brothers released it and it floated hundreds of feet into the air.

The first live passengers in a balloon were a rooster, a duck, and a young sheep. The Montgolfier brothers put them in a basket carrier and filled a huge balloon with hot air from a fire.

This inspired two brave men to risk their lives by being the first humans to leave the ground and fly in the air. One man was the Marquis d'Arlandes; the other was Jean de Rozier, a French doctor.

In a Paris park they tied a basket to the bottom of their beautifully decorated balloon. A roaring fire filled the balloon with hot air.

The two men jumped into the basket and released the ropes. They rose above the heads of the people on the ground for the first human flight. The year was still 1783.

That same year, a French scientist, Jacques Charles, filled a balloon with hydrogen and sent it up into the air. This was to avoid the danger of fire when hot air was used to fill balloons.

Later that year, Charles and a friend, Jean Robert, went up in a balloon that was filled with hydrogen. They also invented a valve that enabled them to come down by letting hydrogen escape from inside the balloon.

WHEN DID AUTOMOBILE RACING BEGIN?

Did you know that the best-attended sporting event in the whole world is the Indianapolis 500 (500-mile race) held each Memorial Day at Speedway, Indiana? Millions of people all over the world watch automobile races every year.

Quite soon after the automobile was developed, different manufacturers became involved in arguments as to who was making the fastest and most durable automobile. This led to the first international auto race in history. It was run in France in 1895, and was a 732-mile race from Paris to Bordeaux and back. The race was won by a French Panhard, traveling at an average speed of 15 miles per hour!

In 1900, James Gordon Bennett put up a trophy for a series of races. The cars that competed had to be entirely the products of the country they represented. This really started international automobile racing.

In 1906, the Automobile Club of France decided to run its own race, the Grand Prix. The cars in this contest took two days to complete 12 laps on a 64-mile course near Le Mans. Grand Prix racing developed from this and there are now such international races in Monaco, Belgium, Holland, France, England, Germany, Italy, Mexico, South Africa, and the United States.

The first important automobile race in the United States was spurred by the success of the race in France from Paris to Bordeaux. It was held in Chicago on November 28, 1895. The object was to test the speed and the stamina of American-made cars. J. Frank Duryea, one of America's leading auto manufacturing pioneers, won in a Duryea car at a speed of 7½ miles per hour.

Today, automobile racing is divided into many groups. There is stock car racing, in which a car must not be over three years old, must resemble a showroom automobile, and must use a stock production engine. There are also sports-car racing and drag racing. In drag racing, the object is to cover a prescribed straightaway distance, usually ¼ of a mile, as quickly as possible. Even drag racing has over 75 classes of cars.

HOW DID KINDERGARTENS START?

Most children start first grade when they are five, six, or seven years old. But many children start going to school before first grade. They attend kindergarten or nursery school.

In the public school system of the United States, kindergarten is the class in elementary school that comes before the first grade. Children in kindergarten are at play most of their day, but they are constantly learning through their play. They learn to plan activities, to follow simple directions, and to adjust to school life.

The idea of schools for the very young began in Europe in the late 1700's and early 1800's. Industry was growing, and many mothers who went to work had to take their youngest children into the factories with them.

One answer to this problem was the development of the infant school. The first infant school was started in Scotland in 1816 by a man called Robert Owen. He set up a system of schools for all the children in a mill town who were under twelve. The very youngest children were placed in an infant school as soon as they had learned to walk.

But even before this, educators had been concerned with the training of young children, and had many theories about this. A German teacher called Friedrich Froebel developed his own theory and method of teaching young children. He opened a school in Blankenburg, Germany, in 1837, and named his school *Kindergarten,* or "children's garden." This was the first kindergarten.

Froebel believed that children expressed their interests through their play. He developed a set of play materials, which he called gifts, for use in the kindergarten. The gifts included six soft, colored balls, and several wooden spheres, cubes, and cylinders. In addition to using the gifts, children in Froebel's kindergarten sang songs, played games, and listened to stories.

Other educators later developed other ways of helping very young children start learning in kindergarten.

WHEN DID FREE EDUCATION START IN AMERICA?

It is hard for today's student to realize how difficult it was to get free schooling for everyone, and to make sure that all children went to school.

Many people thought that poor children did not need to be educated. They insisted that the government had no right to take tax money from one man to educate another man's children. And poor families wanted their children to work, because they needed the money.

In 1647, the colony of Massachusetts passed a school law that required every town with at least fifty families to have an elementary school, and every town with one hundred families to have a Latin grammar school (these were schools that taught reading, writing and Latin, but no science, history, mathematics, or English).

This law marked the beginning of American public education. Other New England colonies passed similar laws. The New Englanders who settled the West took this idea with them.

The New England elementary schools were public schools open to all children. They were built by the town, and some tax money was used to run them. But parents who could afford it had to pay a fee for each child.

Sometimes there was not enough money to keep these schools going. Then parents had to pay if they wanted their children in school. In 1827 Massachusetts passed a law saying that the schools would have to be paid for entirely out of tax money. Most of the other New England states soon followed.

The struggle for tax money to pay for schools went on, state by state. It was not completely won in New York until 1867, and in Pennsylvania until 1868. Public schools in New Jersey were not free until 1871. Delaware, Maryland, and the southern states did not have free education until after the Civil War.

The midwestern states did better, because the Federal Government helped start their school systems. It gave the states free, unsettled land that could be sold for money to start school funds. Before the end of the nineteenth century, there was free education in all the states.

WHERE DID HUMMINGBIRDS ORIGINATE?

Sometimes we hear about strange and interesting creatures that are found far off in exotic lands. Well, one of the most remarkable creatures of all is found right here—a native of North and South America. This is the hummingbird, the smallest and most brilliant of birds.

There are about five hundred different kinds of hummingbirds in South America and sixteen species in western North America. The only hummingbird found east of the Mississippi River is the ruby-throated hummingbird.

The hummingbird gets its name from the humming sound made by its vibrating wings. A hummingbird doesn't fly the way other birds do. Its wings move so rapidly that they cannot be seen clearly by the eye, so that when you look at a hummingbird hovering over a flower, it seems to be suspended in mid-air as if by magic!

A hummingbird has a long tongue that can be folded lengthwise to form a sucking tube. It sticks this tongue into flowers and sucks up the nectar, somewhat the way butterflies do. It eats spiders and insects it finds on plants, and sometimes it captures them on the wing!

The bill of the hummingbird varies with the species. In some cases, the slender bill is shorter than the rest of the head, as with most birds. But some hummingbirds have a bill that is actually longer than the rest of the body. One kind, the sicklebill hummingbird, has a bill that curves downward like a hook.

The ruby-throated hummingbird, which is found in the eastern part of the United States, is only about three-and-a-half inches long, including the bill. It builds a nest shaped like a cup that is only an inch and a half wide! This delicate little nest is made of fine fibers, plant down, and bits of lichens, and is fastened in place with spider webs.

The way the hummingbird feeds its young is interesting, too. After swallowing soft insects and partly digesting them, the mother bird puts her bill into the open beak of the nestling and squirts the food into the young bird's mouth!

HOW DID NATIONAL ANTHEMS ORIGINATE?

A national anthem is a patriotic song that is sung or played on official occasions as a special sign of respect for a country. National anthems and patriotic songs serve to unite a people in their common hopes and ideals.

The origin of many national anthems is unknown. Often a melody was already popular as a folk song when someone set a patriotic text to it. Only a few melodies were actually written to be national anthems. The most famous of these is the anthem of West Germany, which was originally composed for Austria by the great composer Franz Joseph Haydn.

Several older national anthems and patriotic songs have the same melodies but different words. Some of them have even been sung as war songs by opposing armies in the same battle. The British anthem, "God Save the Queen," has provided the melody for patriotic songs in Denmark, Germany, Russia, Switzerland, and all English-

FRANCIS SCOTT KEY

speaking areas of the world. In the United States the words of "America" are sung to this same melody.

"God Save the Queen" first appeared as a tune in 1619. It was written by the English composer John Bull. The first public performance of the anthem took place on September 28, 1745.

The national anthem of the United States was written during the War of 1812. Francis Scott Key, a Baltimore lawyer, was aboard one of the British ships that attacked Fort McHenry. All night long, Key watched the attack. When he saw the American flag at dawn, still flying over the fort, he was so moved that he wrote the words of "The Star-Spangled Banner" on the back of an envelope. For the tune, he had in mind an old English song called "To Anacreon in Heaven."

The "Marseillaise," the French national anthem, was the battle song of the French revolutionary period (1789–1815). The words and music were written by Claude Joseph Rouget de Lisle, a captain in the French Army. It was declared the official national anthem of France in July, 1795.

HOW DID NATIONAL PARKS START?

One of the greatest pleasures in traveling through the United States is to visit a national park or national monument. Just think what a loss it would be to us if these lovely or historic places weren't preserved and guarded and kept up in good condition.

National parks and monuments are areas of great scenic, historic, and scientific importance that have been set aside by the United States Government for the use and enjoyment of the people. Every year millions of people visit the parks, monuments, and other areas that make up the National Park System. The national parks in Canada are also popular with tourists.

The National Park System had its beginning in 1870. A small group of men had just completed a month-long exploration of the Yellowstone region. They were gathered around a campfire, and after hours of discussion the men decided that they should not claim this wonderland for themselves. They felt that it should be set aside for the use and enjoyment of all the people.

So they started a campaign, and two years later, in 1872, an Act of Congress, signed by President Ulysses S. Grant, made the Yellowstone region a "public park or pleasuring ground." This was the first national park in the whole world!

In the years that followed, other beautiful regions of the country were set aside for the people. To manage these parks, the National Park Service was set up by Act of Congress on August 25, 1916.

In a national park, park rangers are on duty at all times to answer questions and to help visitors in any difficulty. Nature walks, guided tours, and campfire talks are offered by specially-trained staff members. The park service also protects the animals and plants within the parks.

WHEN WAS THE CAPITOL IN WASHINGTON BUILT?

In the Capitol Building in Washington, D.C., the Congress of the United States meets to debate bills and make laws. The Capitol is also the site of the Presidential Inauguration.

This huge, impressive building dominates the skyline of Washington. Wide avenues radiate from the Capitol like spokes of a great wheel.

The cornerstone of the Capitol was laid in 1793 by George Washington. The main portion of the building, made of Virginia sandstone, was constructed between 1793 and 1827. The House and Senate wings, built of Massachusetts white marble, were added between 1851 and 1865.

The Capitol's iron dome, which rises to a height of 288 feet, is capped by the Statue of Freedom. This statue, made by the American sculptor Thomas Crawford, was set onto the dome during the Civil War in 1862. Abraham Lincoln watched as it was placed in position and 35 cannons roared in salute. Encircling the base of the dome are 36 columns, representing the states in the Union when the dome was completed.

The Capitol has had several renovations. It was burned by the British in the War of 1812. The fire destroyed the original wooden roofing, much of the Capitol's interior, and many marble columns. Then in 1961 the East Front of the Capitol was remodeled. It is on the steps of the East Front that the President takes his oath on Inauguration Day.

Near the Capitol are the Supreme Court and the Library of Congress. The Court, of white marble, symbolizes the prestige and solemnity of the law. Here, in the highest court of the land, the nine justices of the Supreme Court meet.

WHO DISCOVERED MEDICINE?

A doctor practices medicine—and so the first man who could help someone feel better was really, in a way, the first doctor. For example, a caveman who pulled a thorn out of somebody's finger was doing what a doctor does.

Primitive people practiced a kind of medicine that we would call magic. They used chants or songs, or a stew of herbs and leaves. Or, by accident, they may have discovered that the warmth of a fire eased a sprained shoulder, or an herb drink helped a stomach-ache. Many primitive peoples of today can set and splint a broken bone, or use plants that are laxatives or that will put people to sleep.

But doctors as such seem to have existed from the earliest civilizations. The Babylonians left medical writings describing various diseases so clearly that doctors today can recognize them. The ancient Egyptians had medical treatments, and these included pills and ointments containing drugs. They even performed surgical operations on the outer surfaces of the body.

A man called Aesculapius was the earliest physician in Greek history. He practiced a kind of magic medicine. But gradually true medicine began to develop. A man called Hippocrates, who lived about 400 B.C., did so much to rescue medicine from such magic and superstition that he is called the "Father of Medicine."

In his writings he taught that the physician should observe the patient closely and accurately. He should use gentle treatment and try to encourage the natural healing process. The physician should never risk harming the patient. He should keep the patient's secrets.

Hippocrates also recognized and described many diseases. Some of the medical facts he observed are as true today as they were over two thousand years ago. So perhaps we can call him the world's first doctor in terms of what we mean by that today.

WHO DISCOVERED INSULIN?

Insulin is used for the treatment of a disease called diabetes. When a person has this disease, some fault in his body chemistry keeps it from using starches and sugar to make energy.

A large gland called the pancreas makes a substance called insulin that the body needs to use starches and sugar. The body of a person with diabetes either does not make enough insulin or does not use its insulin. If this disease goes untreated, he suffers from extreme thirst, loses weight, feels weak, and may eventually become unconscious and die.

However, these things need not happen to a person with diabetes now that insulin is manufactured. The diabetic patient can take it by daily injection. With this manufactured insulin and a regular diet, he can lead a normal life.

Doctors had known for some time that a person suffering from diabetes could not make use of the sugar in his body. The problem was how to provide diabetics with insulin. Scientists thought they knew the answer: give a diabetic insulin taken from the pancreas of a healthy animal. But no one had been able to extract insulin.

This was the achievement of Frederick Grant Banting, a Canadian doctor and scientist who was born in 1891 near Alliston, Ontario. He was teaching in London, Ontario, and one evening, while preparing a lecture on the pancreas, he suddenly realized how he might extract insulin. He went to the University of Toronto and asked Professor John Macleod, director of a large laboratory, for help. Macleod agreed to let him use the laboratory for a few weeks.

In May, 1921, with the help of Charles Best, a young graduate student, he set to work. They worked day and night, and within several weeks obtained the first insulin from the pancreas of a dog. By January, 1922, after many tests, they were able to give insulin to a diabetic, a young boy near death. He showed immediate improvement. Other patients given insulin improved, too. An important step forward in medical history had been made.

WHO STARTED THE BOY SCOUTS OF AMERICA?

Many years ago, an American businessman called W. D. Boyce was in London. In the fog, he couldn't find the house of a friend he was looking for, so he stopped a boy who was passing and asked for directions.

The boy not only gave him directions, but guided Mr. Boyce to the house. When the American offered the boy a coin, it was refused. "I am a Boy Scout," the boy said. "Helping you was my daily good turn—Boy Scouts do not accept tips."

Mr. Boyce was so interested by this explanation that he wanted to learn more about Boy Scouts. He went to the London Scout headquarters, where he was told the history of the movement and provided with pamphlets and other printed matter.

He learned that the Boy Scout movement had been founded in England by Lord Baden-Powell when he returned to England after the Boer War. Baden-Powell had become interested in various boys' organizations and had combined their best features with ideas of his own, finally developing the Boy Scout program.

Mr. Boyce was so impressed with what he learned that on February 8, 1910, he incorporated the Boy Scouts of America. Scouts observe this anniversary with much ceremony every year. In 1916 the

Boy Scouts of America were granted a federal charter, because Boy Scouts had been so helpful in many ways in their various communities. The charter gives protection to the name and insignia of scouting and authorizes the members to wear an official uniform.

From the time the Boy Scout movement started in the United States, more than seventeen million boys and leaders have been registered members. There are three age groups in scouting, with programs and activities adapted to the interests of boys at each level. The Cub Scouts are boys eight through ten years of age; the Boy Scouts, eleven through thirteen; and the Explorers, fourteen and up.

HOW DID THE SALVATION ARMY START?

Today there are very few countries in the world where the Salvation Army and its work are not known. Yet this great organization began in the mind of a single man. This man was William Booth.

In 1865 Booth was a young Methodist revivalist who walked the dreariest streets in London's East End. There he prayed for the men and women who gathered around him, though they usually jeered at him and even threw stones.

But Booth refused to be discouraged. Day after day, he went into the streets with his wife and a few followers. Day after day, this small group invited people to come to meetings held in a tent, a dance hall or an old warehouse. During these meetings they tried to bring religion to the poor and to do whatever they could to relieve their misery.

At first the group called themselves the Christian Mission, but in 1878 they organized themselves as the Salvation Army. The organization adopted a kind of "military" system. Its founder, William Booth, was called General, and its workers wore uniforms. It grew with amazing speed.

The Army as a whole is divided into territories, which are made up of divisions, which in turn consist of corps and outposts (mission stations). The General and other international officers operate from the international headquarters in London.

The Salvation Army has set up about eighteen thousand posts throughout the world. At these posts it carries on its social work. Its services include hotels with inexpensive food and lodging, factories, farm colonies, orphanages, rescue homes, day nurseries, insurance societies, and so on.

The Salvation Army was organized in the United States by George Scott Railton in 1880. Evangeline Booth, daughter of William Booth, became the Commander in the United States in 1904, and in 1934 she became the first woman General of the Salvation Army.

WHEN WERE THE FIRST FIRE FIGHTERS ORGANIZED?

Man has always known that fire can be his friend and servant, and can also be a great destroyer. Primitive man, however, didn't have the problem of fighting fires as we have, simply because he didn't live in houses that were grouped together—in other words, in villages, towns, and cities.

But when men began to live together in large groups, they had to concern themselves with the problem of fighting fires. And so, long before Christ (in fact, many centuries before), fire brigades were organized. They existed in many cities throughout the world. The ancient Romans had fire brigades to protect the city, and used slaves for this work.

By the way, the Romans also developed the first means of throwing a continuous stream of water. Roman firemen used axes, blankets, buckets, ladders, and poles! In the Middle Ages there was some organized fire fighting here and there, but it was not very efficient.

Fire fighting as we know it was started in England. It came about because fire-insurance companies were organized, and they, of course, were interested in cutting down the loss from fires and preventing their spread. The officials of London hadn't done much about this problem, so the insurance companies organized fire brigades of their own.

Probably the first such brigade was organized in 1722, and then others followed. These insurance companies would place fire marks on the buildings they insured, and probably didn't bother too much with other buildings. In 1833 the first organized fire fighting system for the city of London was set up.

In the United States, as in most parts of the world, before the local authorities (of the city or town) set up fire brigades, the citizens themselves would organize volunteer fire fighters. In fact, the job of fighting fires is still done mostly by volunteers. There are about one million fire fighters in the United States—and only one out of ten is a paid fireman working full time!

WHEN DID LABOR UNIONS BEGIN?

In ancient Greece and Rome slaves did much of the labor. Food and shelter were provided by their masters in return. During the Middle Ages, serfs were required to work for the lord of the manor in return for protection. Laborers were tillers of the soil, not wage earners.

As trade increased, the town replaced the feudal manor as the principal place where people worked. Merchants and artisans organized into associations, or guilds, for each craft. These artisans and craftsmen worked at home or in small shops, and there were a few factories with many workers laboring together.

This was all changed toward the end of the eighteenth century with the coming of the Industrial Revolution. As machines were developed that could produce more goods faster than the individual worker, factories were built to house the machines. Handwork and small shops all but disappeared. The worker had to seek a job from an employer, and he was paid in wages for his services. And when workers had problems, they had no one who would listen to them.

Conditions in the early English cotton mills were particularly bad. So the workers began to organize into unions. They felt that if they stood together, their grievances and complaints had a better chance of a fair hearing.

These trade unions were founded in the towns as small clubs of skilled craftsmen. In 1868 the Trades Union Congress, the first big and successful union organization, was formed in Manchester, England.

There was a great need for unions in the early days of the American Republic, but they were hard to organize and public opinion was against them. The first union in the United States was formed in 1792 by eight shoemakers in Philadelphia. It did not last a year.

During the early years of the nineteenth century, unions began to form city-wide trade associations. The first was the Mechanics' Union of Trade Associations. It was founded in Philadelphia in 1828. The first important national labor federation was formed in 1866.

HOW OLD IS WEAVING?

Weaving is the method by which threads are interlaced to make cloth. The principles of weaving have not changed through the ages. Modern textile mills do quickly on machines what ancient peoples did slowly by hand.

Cavemen, who lived about thirty thousand years ago, learned how to weave. They used straw, stalks of reed, or other materials to weave baskets. Nets for fishing and the capture of game were also woven by man in prehistoric times.

What these ancient peoples didn't realize was that cords, which are really yarns, could be interlaced to make soft fabrics or cloths. The idea of weaving cloth seems to have developed in certain particular places and then spread all over the world.

The most ancient woven cloths that we have records of are these: the Near East, about 5000 B.C.; Egypt, about 4000 B.C.; central Europe, about 2500 B.C.; China, about 1200 B.C.; and the Peruvian coast of South America, about 1500 B.C.

The use of different fibers for weaving developed in various places according to what was available. Wool was first used when the sheep was domesticated, about 1600 B.C. Cotton was first used in India and spread from there through Asia and finally to Europe.

Silk fibers were first used in China. On the other side of the world, in ancient Peru, the cotton plant and llamas and alpacas were providing material for making cloth. And since man has always liked to have colorful clothing, it is interesting to know that the ancient Peruvians had already found ways to have more than 150 tints and shades in their cloth.

Today, of course, most weaving is done in mills. But in many cases the weaving of rugs and tapestries is still done by hand by skillful artists.

WHEN WAS THE FIRST POTTERY MADE?

Wet clay can be modeled into almost any shape. After a few days the clay becomes dry and hard. If the clay is baked, or fired, the nature of the clay changes. It can no longer be made soft and workable. Objects made of baked clay are called ceramics. Ceramic vessels (containers) are called pottery.

The first pottery was made about ten thousand years ago. To keep grain from spilling through the holes in baskets, the insides were smeared with wet clay. Perhaps one day a basket of this kind fell unnoticed on a campfire. The reeds burned away, and the first piece of pottery had been made.

There are three kinds of pottery—earthenware, stoneware, and porcelain. The simplest kind of pottery is made from clay and then fired. It is called earthenware. It is porous, and water will slowly leak out of it.

As time passed, people learned that certain rocks could be melted into a kind of glass. The rocks were crushed to a fine powder and mixed with clay. The pottery made from this clay is called stoneware. Stoneware, which does not leak, can be used over a fire for cooking.

During the Tang dynasty (618–906 A.D.) the Chinese began to make another kind of pottery. It was made from a special white clay mixed with powdered rock. This pottery, called porcelain, was fired in a kiln almost hot enough to melt iron. Porcelain is translucent (light can be seen through it) and hard.

About 3300 B.C., the potter's wheel came into use. The potter puts a ball of wet clay onto the center of the wheel. As the wheel spins, the potter shapes the clay by pressing it with his fingers. Pots made on wheels are always round.

All the ancient civilizations—Egyptians, Persians, Mesopotamians—made beautiful pottery. The Egyptians used glazes of many colors. The Persians painted on their pottery as far back as 4000 B.C. The ancient Greeks and Romans also made large pottery vases. But it was the Chinese who made the most beautiful pottery in ancient times.

WHO PAINTED THE FIRST PICTURES?

The first artists on earth were the cavemen. On the walls of caves in southern France and Spain there are colored drawings of animals that were made from 30,000 to 10,000 B.C.

Many of these drawings are amazingly well-preserved, because the caves were sealed up for many centuries. Early man drew the wild animals that he saw all around him. Very crude human figures, drawn in lifelike positions, have been found in Africa and eastern Spain.

The cave artists filled the cave walls with drawings in rich, bright colors. The pigments used were earth ochers (iron oxides varying in color from light yellow to deep orange) and manganese (a metallic element). These were crushed into a fine powder, mixed with grease, like animal fat, and put on with some sort of brush.

Sometimes the pigments were used in sticks, like crayons. The grease mixed with the powdered pigments made the paint fluid and the pigment particles stuck together. The cavemen must have made brushes out of animal hairs or plants, and sharp tools out of flint for drawing and scratching lines.

One of the first civilizations was developed in Egypt, and they had artists who painted pictures. Much Egyptian art was created for the pyramids and tombs of kings and other important people. Artists recorded scenes from the life of the person in wall paintings in the burial chamber. They used watercolor paints and washes.

Another early civilization, the Aegean, also developed the art of painting to a surprising degree. Their artists had a free and graceful style, and they painted sea life, animals, flowers, athletic games, and processionals. Their paintings were made on wet plaster walls, a kind of painting we now call fresco.

So you see that painting goes back to the very earliest times of man and civilization.

WHEN WAS SCULPTURE FIRST CREATED?

It may be that sculpture is the oldest of the arts. People carved before they painted or even designed homes.

Only a few objects survive to show what sculpture was like thousands of years ago. But people living today in primitive societies often carve things that may be similar to prehistoric sculpture.

Prehistoric sculpture was never made to be beautiful. It was always made to be used in rituals. Figures of men, women, and animals were made to honor the forces of nature, which were worshipped as evil or good spirits.

The earliest civilizations of man also used sculpture to express their beliefs. The ancient Egyptians believed in life after death, and they carved life-size and even larger statues of their rulers, nobles, and gods. They were placed in tombs, and the Egyptians believed the spirit of the dead person would return to these images.

One of the greatest periods in the history of sculpture came with the Greek civilization that started about 600 B.C. For the Greeks, sculpture became one of their most important forms of expression.

The Greeks made the human figure the principal object of their art. Sculptors in Greece were always looking for better ways to represent the human figure.

During the first one thousand years of Christianity, very little sculpture was produced. But after the year 1000, and for the next three centuries, some of the most impressive Christian churches were built and much great sculpture was created for these churches.

Later on, during the Renaissance, the human figure was again glorified and great sculptors produced masterpieces that are among the world's greatest treasures.

HOW DID POETRY ORIGINATE?

First of all, what is poetry? Poetry is language that is deeply felt and deeply moving, written or spoken in a special form. The rhythm of a poem is what makes it different from prose.

From this we can get an idea of how poetry began. Of course, we can never know who first created it or where. But because we know something of the way primitive people acted, we can guess at the beginnings of poetry.

Man had some sort of rhythmic dance even before he had a language. He made sounds and gestures and uttered grunts and cries at special times, such as before a battle or a hunt. Also, he created a drum on which he could beat in many ways. And soon he was using sounds and the drums to send magic words to his gods.

Primitive man then began to develop the dance, and it became more and more complicated as it advanced. Soon the words of the chant to the gods became more important than just sounds from the drum. The words could be understood. In time, the leading performer of such a ceremony was actually a kind of poet, or bard.

WHERE WAS THE FIRST THEATER?

The theater as we know it took a long time to develop. The idea of drama itself had its beginnings in religion.

The Chinese first performed dramalike dances in their temples. Later a playhouse was used. It was just a platform without curtains or changes of lights that had a roof decorated like the roof of a temple.

The Japanese also developed a form of theater in ancient times. One type of drama was called *No,* and a popular form of drama was called *Kabuki.* They were performed on a platform with a temple roof.

In ancient India, dramatic performances were given on specially-built raised platforms, with draperies as background.

The ancient Greeks developed a very great form of drama. The audience was seated on a hillside. The action of the play took place in a grassy circle. There was a building called the *skene,* which was used for the entrances of the actors, for dressing, and for scenic background.

During the Middle Ages, the Christian church condemned all forms of drama, but later religious drama became an important part of church life. Priests in the Middle Ages acted out bible stories as part of the church services.

During the reign of Elizabeth I, the theater in England took a great step forward. In 1576 an actor, James Burbage, built the first playhouse. It was known simply as "the Theatre" and was patterned after the stages that used to be set up in inn courtyards.

Soon other theaters were built, and these included the Globe, where many of Shakespeare's plays were performed; the Red Bull; and the Blackfriars. The audience stood in the pit, in front or around the sides of the stage, or were seated in boxes around and above the stage. Our modern theater had its beginnings with these early English theaters.

HOW DID THE ORCHESTRA DEVELOP?

An orchestra is a large group of musicians playing many kinds of instruments. The standard orchestra has at least seventy-five to one hundred players. Of these, more than half play stringed instruments, which form the foundation of an orchestra. The rest play woodwind, brass, and percussion instruments.

An orchestra such as this is called a symphony orchestra. An orchestra that has fifteen to thirty players is called a chamber orchestra. It is small enough to play in a small hall or "chamber." A string orchestra is made up of only the stringed instruments of the symphony orchestra.

The modern symphony orchestra developed over hundreds of years. There were many experiments and changes, and it was actually the composers of music who had a great deal to do with shaping the orchestra.

The first great pioneer in writing for the orchestra was the Italian, Claudio Monteverdi (1567–1643). He was also the first great composer of opera. In one of his works he used an orchestra of thirty-five musicians playing violas, guitars, harpsichords, organs, trumpets, trombones, and flutes.

When the violin was perfected in the seventeenth century, the strings became the leading instruments of the orchestra. The great French opera composer Rameau (1683–1764) was one of the first composers to use clarinets in the orchestra. He also used bassoons and horns regularly.

Turkish bands traveling in Europe introduced several new percussion instruments. These included the bass drum, triangle, cymbals, and others in this family. So we see how the orchestra grew in terms of the kinds and the number of instruments composers could use. And composers wrote music designed to get new sounds and tone color from the orchestra.

The first orchestra in the United States, still in existence, was the New York Philharmonic, founded in 1842. The Boston Symphony was founded in 1881.

WHEN DID BALLET DANCING BEGIN?

What is a ballet? It is a kind of theatrical entertainment that combines several things: dancing, stage design, and music. Some ballets tell a story, but others just depict an idea or mood.

When you see a ballet, you see the human body performing in the most elegant and harmonious way possible. And it takes strict and strenuous training to enable the dancers to look natural and beautiful as they perform.

Ballet is nearly five hundred years old. It began in Italy about the time Columbus discovered America. It was quite different then from what it is today. At that time ballet was a form of court entertainment. Italian noblemen amused themselves and their guests by combining dancing, music, pantomime, poetry and drama.

So the first ballet dancers were the royalty and nobles of the court, since there were no professional dancers. The steps were modeled on the elegant and rather simple court dances of the day, and the dancers didn't wear toe slippers. However, dancing of this kind was not called ballet until almost one hundred years later at the court of King Henry III of France.

In 1581 Queen Catherine de Médicis ordered a grand entertainment to celebrate a royal wedding. The result was a spectacular ballet. There were hundreds of dancers, singers, and actors. The Italian musician de Beaujoyeulx organized it. He was probably the first choreographer, or maker of dances, as we know the word today. He called his work *The Queen's Comic Ballet,* and ever since performances of this kind have been called ballets.

The leading lady in a ballet company is called a prima ballerina. The first of these was a woman called Lafontaine, who danced in 1681. Later on, various individuals introduced changes and improvements in ballet.

CHAPTER 3
THE
HUMAN BODY

WHAT IS LIFE?

This is probably one of the deepest questions man can ask and one of the greatest mysteries facing him.

Scientists have discovered that all living things are made of a material called protoplasm. They can make a chemical formula for protoplasm, and they can take molecules of various elements and compounds and put them together and make materials like protoplasm. But the materials they make are not alive!

All man can do is examine the living creatures on earth, in all sizes and shapes and wherever they live, and find what it is they have in common. Then we can say that these common qualities make up life.

Let's see what these qualities are. All living things must be able to grow. They grow to a fairly definite size and shape. A kitten becomes a cat; an acorn becomes an oak tree. For some living things it takes a short time to grow to full size; a redwood tree may take thousands of years. But all living things grow.

All living things can replace and repair parts of themselves. A lobster can grow a new claw, human beings can grow new skin or bones, trees grow new leaves.

Another characteristic shared by living things, and living things only, is the ability to reproduce. If this ability didn't exist, living things would disappear from the earth as they grew old and died. Animals, fish, birds, insects, plants—all produce offspring.

Living things are able to adapt to their environment. Man can do this better than any other creatures because of his brain. But plants can do this only to a limited extent.

Living things can also respond to stimuli. This means if something outside of themselves affects them they can react. When you smell food, you respond, and flowers grow toward the light.

This doesn't tell you what life is, but it does describe the qualities that things must have to be considered "alive."

WHY MUST WE BREATHE?

We all know instinctively that we must breathe. But why is it necessary for all living plants and animals to breathe? The reason is a very simple one. By breathing we take in air that provides oxygen. Without this gas, no life can exist.

When we exhale the air, it has changed. As it made its way through our system, some of the oxygen was used up, while the amounts of carbon dioxide and water were increased.

Nature keeps up a constant supply of oxygen for our breathing. In fact, from year to year, there is little change in the amounts of oxygen and carbon dioxide found in the air. This is because the carbon dioxide we breathe out into the air is taken in by plants. They breathe out oxygen, which we need.

Breathing, or respiration, is made up of two parts: external and internal breathing. External breathing is what most of us think of when we refer to breathing. It consists of inhaling and exhaling, or inspiration and expiration. Inspiration means taking in air through the mouth, the nose, or both. Expiration means sending out air through those same channels, but air that has had about one-fifth of its oxygen exchanged for an equal amount of carbon dioxide. This happens in the lungs.

Internal breathing is the opposite of external. The oxygen taken from the air in the lungs is carried to the tissues of the body by the red cells in the blood. In the tissues this oxygen burns certain food products, making them available for use by the body. The blood takes away the waste products, including water and carbon dioxide. These are returned in the blood to the lungs for exhaling.

Since an exchange of gases (oxygen and carbon dioxide) takes place both in the lungs and in the tissues, a large surface is needed to make this possible. The linings of the lungs of an adult, for example, are equal to a space about 36 feet square. This is larger than the ceiling space of one floor of an average house! Much of this area is kept in reserve, since we might need 8 or 10 times as much oxygen during work as we need at rest. If we need more oxygen, we breathe more deeply or more quickly.

Different creatures breathe at different rates, depending on the oxygen they need.

A newborn baby breathes about once a second, but at the age of 15, breathing is about 20 times a minute. An elephant breathes 10 times a minute; a dog, 25 times a minute.

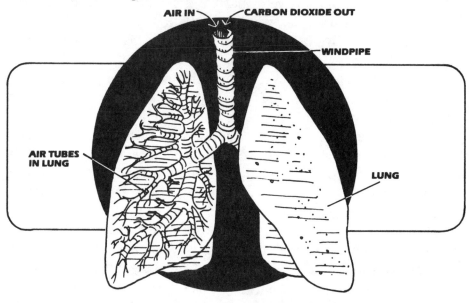

WHAT KEEPS THE HEART BEATING?

As most of us know, the heart is a pump. It drives the blood through the body, thus making life possible.

But what an amazing pump it is! With each beat of the heart, it sends out about one hundred cubic centimeters of blood. In the course of a day this amounts to about 10,567 quarts of blood that are pumped through the blood vessels. In an average lifetime, a heart pumps about 264,175,000 quarts of blood!

Each beat of the human heart lasts about eight-tenths of a second. The heart beats about one hundred thousand times a day, and rests an equal number of times between beats. So it rests about six hours total per day.

Now, what we call the "beat" of the heart is a contracting and a relaxing. During the contracting the blood is pumped out; during the relaxing new blood enters. But this doesn't take place in a simple way as, for example, you might open and close your fist. The contraction takes place in a kind of wave that starts at the bottom of the heart and moves up toward the top.

What keeps the heart beating? Does this impulse to contract and relax come from somewhere else? Is it self-starting? It is one of the most fascinating questions in biology, and much about it still remains a mystery. Let me tell you about an interesting experiment that has been known about for hundreds of years.

Suppose you take a chicken egg and incubate it about twenty-six hours. Now you open it and with a magnifying glass study those cells in the egg from which the chick's heart will later develop. You will see those cells beating! Even before those cells have become a heart, they are already beating!

Now suppose you remove this mass of cells and allow them to grow in a medium. If you cut the growing heart into six pieces, each piece continues to contract for some time! What is the explanation? We don't know. All we can say, it seems, is that the heart has a certain characteristic of automatically contracting. And one of the secrets of life—why it keeps beating—remains a riddle!

WHAT IS HEREDITY?

Every new organism, whether it is a plant, fish, animal, or human, resembles its parents—and yet it differs from them. For example, children may look like one parent or the other, but usually they have some features of each parent. What has happened is that the parents have passed down to the children certain characteristics. The children have "inherited" them. So heredity is the study of how offspring resemble their parents.

The unit of heredity is called the "gene." Genes are large molecules found in the nuclei of both sperm cells and egg cells. Within the nucleus of each cell are long, thin strands, or threads. They are called "chromosomes," and they carry the genes.

Since chromosomes occur in pairs, their genes are also paired. The chromosomes of a cell may contain hundreds of thousands of pairs of genes. Each gene pair controls one or more features of the organism, such as color of hair, shape of nose, size of body, and so on.

There are many "laws" of heredity, which means that the process takes place in certain ways. For example, every trait that is inherited depends on a single "factor," and each factor behaves independently. Because a certain trait is inherited from the parents, it doesn't mean that any other trait will also necessarily be inherited. In other words, the factors, or genes, have nothing to do with each other.

Some genes carry traits that are "dominant," and others carry traits that are "recessive." For example, the gene for curly hair seems to be dominant to the gene for straight hair. When both parents are curly-haired, they usually have curly-haired children. But if each parent carries a recessive gene for straight hair, some children may be straight-haired.

Scientists have studied such human traits as color of eyes, hair, and skin, so that they usually can tell how they will be inherited by people whose family history is known for several generations.

WHY ARE SOME PEOPLE SMARTER THAN OTHERS?

One thing everybody seems to realize is that some people seem to be bright and intelligent, and others seem to be backward and learn slowly. But not everybody agrees as to why this is so.

We do know that many cases of low mental ability are the result of injuries at birth, glandular disorders occurring before or after birth, or diseases that have caused damage to the brain. In many cases the causes of retarded mental development cannot be determined.

There is a great deal of disagreement among experts as to the influence of heredity on intelligence. Some believe that in most cases a child inherits his intelligence. Others think that a child's intelligence is a result of the experiences he has had and the kind of environment in which he has lived.

Probably both of these opinions are partially true. The most common belief is that a child inherits a capacity for mental growth. But the degree to which he develops within that capacity depends upon a great many factors in his environment. There are perhaps many people who could have developed higher mental abilities if during childhood they had had better opportunities.

How is intelligence measured? What is really measured is "mental age." This is done through a series of mental tests. For example, most children of six years can do the problems and perform the tasks required in a certain test. A few four and five-year-olds can also do them. On the other hand, there may be children of ten or twelve years of age, or even adults, for whom they are too difficult.

The first group are "average," the second group are "superior," and the third, "retarded." If a child passes enough tests so that his average is that of a six-year-old, his mental age is said to be six years.

If a six-year-old has a mental age of six years, his intelligence quotient (IQ) is 100. If a five-year-old has a mental age of six, his IQ is 120. IQ's above 110 are generally considered superior.

HOW DOES THE BRAIN STORE INFORMATION?

Storing information is remembering, and remembering is closely linked to learning.

Psychologists have tried to explain how people remember and why they forget many of the things they learn. No one has yet found all the answers. It is believed, according to one theory, that when a person learns something, a physical change of some kind takes place. A trace, or pattern, is left in the brain. And it is believed that memories, or the traces memory may leave in the brain, simply fade away in the course of time.

The way you feel about a particular experience may also determine whether you remember or forget it. In general, people are apt to forget things that are unpleasant or upsetting and remember things that are pleasant.

Brains can learn different kinds of tasks. Better-developed brains can learn more complicated tasks. In the simplest brains, learning is very crude. Humans show the greatest learning abilities.

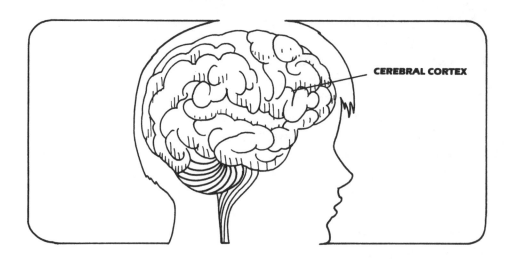

CEREBRAL CORTEX

But how and where does the brain store the information that we call memory? As we said, scientists are not yet able to fully explain it. In the human brain, areas of the cortex appear to be involved. The cortex is the twisted, wrinkled, and knotted surface of the largest part of the brain (the cerebrum).

When these areas are excited by weak electrical currents, a person "relives" past experiences. These stimuli force the brain to reproduce experiences that are stored within it from the past. And it is known that injury to certain areas of the brain will result in loss of memory.

But are these the places in the brain where the information is stored? We don't know. Nor do we know how the information is stored. Some scientists think that storing information is a chemical process—the individual nerve cells have chemically-coded information within them. Other scientists believe that memory is the result of some permanent change in the structure of the nerve. So memory is still a mystery!

WHAT IS MULTIPLE SCLEROSIS?

It is always unpleasant to read about diseases that afflict people, but they are part of our knowledge of man and how he lives.

Multiple sclerosis is a disorder of the brain and nervous system. It usually develops early in adult life, and it seems to attack people who

116

are otherwise healthy. The disease often stops and then reappears again, and it may last over a period of years.

What happens in this disease is that certain matter in the nervous system, in the spinal cord, and in the brain is destroyed. This happens in tiny spots scattered through the nervous system.

Because this disease shows up in many different symptoms and fluctuates so much, it is hard to diagnose. Often, at the beginning of multiple sclerosis there is a temporary mistiness of vision. There may be no pain, and the person doesn't become blind. In fact, this symptom may be so mild that the person may let it pass without going to a doctor.

Then later the person begins to have double vision and a tingling or burning sensation in the skin. The patient may also not be able to coordinate his movements, and he may feel weak and may shake or even begin to stammer. In some cases, the person starts to talk in a strange way, slurring his speech, or talking monotonously.

Eventually, the muscles of the legs become stiff or have spasms. In some patients there are also mental symptoms. The mind doesn't seem able to work well. And a person may be very depressed or very elated.

When a case is far advanced, the patient may become very aggressive. A curious thing is that the most common symptom is that the person feels everything is fine; he is very optimistic even though he has severe symptoms. He might smile or giggle frequently.

At present there is no known cure for multiple sclerosis.

WHAT IS A PHOBIA?

Did you ever know anybody who was afraid of high places, or someone who was afraid of closed places? There are people who are afraid of crowds, or of being touched by others. There is a name for behaving this way: it is called a "phobic reaction," and we say the person has a "phobia."

Is something "wrong" with such people? Are they "sick" in some way? No—but we might say they are suffering from some emotional disturbance. Something upsets them—or has upset them in the past—

very strongly. And such a person is trying to deal with this emotional disturbance—it can be called "emotional pain"—just as you would try to deal with physical pain.

We all react to emotional upsets. We cry, we blush, we might break out in a sweat. But some people, who feel this emotional stress more strongly, or whose power of resistance is weaker, try to deal with this emotional pain in an unnatural, unusual way. This kind of reaction is sometimes called "neurotic."

One such way of reacting is to develop a phobia, which is unreasonable fear of a specific thing, such as fear of high places, or closed-in places. An interesting thing about a phobia is that the thing the person is afraid of is usually a thing or situation he can avoid. After all, nobody forces people to climb to high places or get into closed places. And as long as a person can avoid these things, he feels fine. He doesn't have what is called "anxiety."

But why should a particular person have a fear of high places, to take an example? The truth is, he is really afraid of something else, or perhaps felt afraid of something else when he was a child. It might have been his father whom he loved and feared at the same time. He didn't want to admit he was afraid of his father, so he substituted a fear of high places, which is a symbol of his father. And since he can avoid high places, he can avoid facing the fact that he is afraid of his father. All of this seems very complicated, doesn't it? But then the human being and how he behaves is a very complicated matter!

WHAT HAPPENS TO THE WATER WE DRINK?

You may think that when you drink a glass of water it goes bubbling through your body and out as if it were going through a pipe. But water and your body are involved in a much more complicated way.

An adult man takes in about two quarts of water a day as fluids, and he takes in another quart from what we call "solid" foods. Fruit, vegetables, bread, and meat are really 30 to 90 percent water! Besides these three quarts he takes in from the outside, in his body about ten quarts of water pass back and forth between the different systems and

organs. For example, every time you swallow, you swallow some saliva. In the next few moments, a quantity of water equal to that saliva will pass from the blood vessels into the salivary glands to replace the water you swallowed! The swallowed water returns from the stomach and the intestines to the blood. And so the ten quarts of water in your body are circulating between the blood and the organs every day!

A man has about five quarts of blood in his blood vessels, and three of them are water. His blood vessels will continue to have these three quarts of water no matter what he does. He may be "dried out" after a long hike, or he may have drunk four quarts of beer at a party —there will still be three quarts of water in his blood! And even if a man could drink ten quarts of water at a time, he could not dilute his blood; it keeps that balance of water and solids all the time.

What happens when you drink a certain quantity of water? One-fourth of it goes to the intestine; one-fourth goes into the liver; one-fourth goes into the muscles; and the last fourth goes to the kidneys and bladder. The muscles are the largest water reservoir you have in your body. In a grown man, the muscles can take in and hold up to thirty quarts of water!

When the liver gives up water to the blood, it stimulates the kidney to excrete water. This fills up the bladder, and we get rid of the excess water.

WHAT MAKES YOUR VOICE CHANGE?

The kind of voice you have depends chiefly on your vocal cords. These vocal cords are made of elastic fibers. You might compare them to the very best violin strings.

The vocal cords can be made tense or slack. In fact, your vocal cords can be in any of about 170 different positions. When a column of air (which you push upward) strikes the vocal cords, they begin to vibrate. This vibration produces sound waves.

If the vocal cords are slack, they may vibrate about eighty times per second and the result is deep tones. If they are tensed, they vibrate rapidly, perhaps one thousand times a second, and produce short sound waves or high tones.

A child has short vocal cords. So they produce short air waves and a child has a high-pitched voice. As a child grows, the vocal cords become longer. As they become longer, the voice becomes deeper. The average length of a man's vocal cords is greater than that of a woman's, which is why men's voices are deeper.

In boys, growth often takes place so quickly, and the whole larynx changes so quickly, that they can't get used to it and can't control it perfectly. That's why we often have "the breaking of the voice" with young boys.

While the general pitch of an adult's voice depends on the length of the vocal cords, each voice has a certain range. It is this range that determines what kind of voice the person has. Voices can be divided into six groups: bass, baritone, and tenor for men, and alto, mezzo-soprano, and soprano for women.

The quality of a human voice, however, depends on many other things as well, especially the resonating spaces such as windpipe, lungs, nasal cavities, and so on. People with beautiful voices have resonating spaces shaped a certain way and know how to control them.

HOW ARE DEAF-MUTES TAUGHT TO SPEAK?

Until the sixteenth century, deaf-mutes were treated very cruelly. They were regarded as idiots, incapable of intelligence, and were locked up in asylums or even killed. But in the sixteenth century, an Italian doctor named Jerome Cardan got the idea of teaching deaf-mutes through written characters.

As the result of his work, about a hundred years later a finger alphabet was developed, similar to the finger alphabet used today. With the finger alphabet, a deaf-mute makes the letters with his fingers and spells out words. He also depends on sign language. For example, sweeping the forefinger across the lips means "You are not telling me the truth." A tap on the chin with three fingers means "My uncle." With this alphabet some deaf-mutes can spell out as many as 130 words a minute!

But many teachers of deaf-mutes believe that the use of sign language and the finger alphabet is not the best method. It forces the deaf-mute to communicate only with other people in the same condition. So these teachers use a method known as "oral instruction." In this method the deaf are taught to understand what is spoken to them, and even to speak themselves.

Nowadays many of the deaf and hard-of-hearing learn to interpret what is said by watching the lips of the speaker. They learn to speak themselves by observing and feeling the lips and vocal organs of the teacher and then imitating the motions.

Hearing aids are being used more and more. In schools and classes for deaf and hard-of-hearing children, group hearing aids are used. The group hearing aids have individual earphones for each child so that the volume and tone can be adjusted. The teacher speaks through a microphone, and the children hear her in the same manner as if they were listening to a radio with earphones.

WHY DO HUMANS HAVE HAIR ON THEIR BODIES?

Birds have feathers, and mammals, such as man, have hair. It is believed that feathers and hair enabled birds and mammals to develop far beyond their common ancestors, the reptiles.

In human beings, there are only two parts of the body where there is no hair: the palms of the hand and the soles of the feet. The hair on the rest of the body is believed to be a leftover from the coat of heavy hair that our prehistoric ancestors had.

When a human baby is about a hundred days old in the mother's body, a thick coat of hair sprouts from the skin. After another hundred days, these hairs are shed. This is called the embryonal hair.

This hair is replaced by the delicate hair of a newborn baby. Then this hair is transformed at the time of puberty (about fourteen years in boys and twelve years in girls) into the final coat of hair that the person will have.

The development of the adult coat of hair is regulated by the sex glands. In males, certain hormones promote the development of hair on the face and body, and keep down the growth of hair on the head. The female hormones act in just the opposite way.

Why we need this hair is not quite understood by science. We can say that the hair of the eyebrows, lashes, ears, and nose, are probably there to protect us against dust and insects. A man's beard, in prehistoric times, probably helped set men apart from women—even at a distance—and helped give the man an appearance of power. According to Charles Darwin, the fine hairs of the body help us to shed perspiration and water.

An adult male has from three hundred thousand to five hundred thousand hairs in his skin. Blond persons with finer hair have the most hair; red-haired people, who have the coarsest hair, have the fewest hairs on their bodies.

WHAT MAKES OUR MUSCLES TIRED?

Muscles are the "movers" of the body. For every bone that can move, there are muscles to move it. Muscles are firmly anchored to the bones.

They move a bone by pulling it. A muscle pulls because it has the ability to contract; that is, to make itself shorter and fatter. When it contracts, it pulls.

When a muscle contracts, or pulls, it produces lactic acid. This acid is like a fatigue poison—it is the chief reason the muscles feel tired. For example, when lactic acid is removed from a tired muscle, that muscle is able to go to work again. So in the course of a day, by using our muscles, we "poison" ourselves with lactic acid. We become tired.

There are other substances in the body that make us feel tired. They are called fatigue toxins, and they are created in the body when we carry on muscular activity. The blood carries these toxins through the body so that not just the muscles feel tired, but the whole body does, especially the brain.

An interesting experiment shows how the lactic acid and toxins are involved with tiredness. A dog is made to work until it is so tired it falls asleep from exhaustion. The blood from that dog is then transfused into a dog that is feeling perky and fresh. The second dog will become tired and fall asleep right in the middle of the transfusion! And it works the opposite way—blood from a wide-awake dog will wake up a tired, sleeping dog.

Why does all this tiredness occur in the body? Because the cells of the body need rest. When we are tired and resting, damages to cells are repaired, nerve cells of the brain recharge their batteries, the joints are lubricated by fluids, and so on.

Sometimes a person who is involved in some athletic activity suddenly seems about to collapse. He feels weak and can hardly breathe. This is exhaustion, and is really almost like a kind of paralysis. The cause of such exhaustion is not known, but it may be produced by an excess of the lactic acid and other fatigue toxins.

WHAT ARE SPRAINS, STRAINS, AND BRUISES?

If you were to play in a rough football game, or get into a fight, you might emerge with sprains, strains, and bruises. What causes them, and what should be done about them?

A sprain is an injury to a joint, such as the ankle, knee, or wrist. In a sprain, the ligaments are stretched or torn. This is usually caused by stretching, twisting, or pressure at the joint. One symptom of a sprain is swelling over the joint, which appears very quickly. You also can't use the joint without increasing pain, and it may look discolored. Since a joint may also be fractured, it shouldn't be used until it has been properly examined. Sometimes it takes longer for a sprain to heal than a simple break in a bone!

A strain is a different kind of injury. In a strain it is the muscle or tendon that is injured. This usually comes from some severe exertion, such as lifting a heavy object from an awkward position.

The symptoms of a strain are stiffness and pain in the part that is affected. The first thing to do for a person who has received a strain is to make him comfortable so that the injured muscles are relaxed. In some cases, heat application and gentle massage will provide some relief by stimulating the circulation. Always rub the affected part in an upward direction. Rubbing alcohol may help in the gentle massage to "loosen up" the tightened muscles.

A bruise is still another kind of injury. It is caused by a blow to some part of the body that breaks the small blood vessels under the skin. As the blood collects in the tissues, it causes swelling and discoloration. A cold cloth may help to prevent discoloration, reduce the swelling, and relieve pain. But usually no treatment is needed for minor bruises. If the skin is broken, a bruise should be treated as any other open wound.

Maybe the best idea of all is simply to be careful when you play or exercise so that you can avoid sprains, strains, and bruises!

WHAT IS ARTHRITIS?

The word arthritis is used to describe a great variety of diseases, all of which affect adversely the joints of the body.

The two most common types of arthritis are degenerative arthritis and rheumatoid arthritis. In degenerative arthritis the aging process of the body is involved. In rheumatoid arthritis there is inflammation, and usually some crippling of the body occurs.

In degenerative arthritis there is no fever, no loss of weight, no general stiffening of the joints or deformity of the body. The joint does not become inflamed. It is a disease of advancing years, and usually begins after forty. The cartilage of the bones becomes worn away and broken, so that surfaces of the bone come in direct contact with each other. This is because cartilage acts as a sort of shock absorber of the joints.

The symptoms are either stiffness or pain when there is movement. Knobs begin to appear at the end joints of the first and second fingers. There is also usually pain and stiffness of the knee.

Rheumatoid arthritis is popularly known as rheumatism. What happens here is that the joints become inflamed. The membrane that lines the joint becomes enlarged, and this eats into the cartilage underneath.

At the same time, the bone below the cartilage begins to change. It loses its mineral substances, and the joint becomes stiff. In time, this can end in loss of motion altogether in the joint, so that the person becomes crippled.

What brings on this type of arthritis is still not fully understood by medical science. There are many theories about it, and one is that it is caused by infection. Victims of arthritis have long been hoping for some cure or magic "pill" that would end their suffering. But none has yet been found. Medical authorities want people to realize that the cause of this arthritis is still unknown, and that even some of the drugs that seem to help only give relief while the drugs are being used. When they are stopped, the symptoms return. And the damaged tissue is not repaired.

CAN WE CONTROL OUR HUNGER AND THIRST?

When you feel thirsty, you have a dry sensation in your throat. And when you feel hungry, you may have the sensation that your stomach is empty. But the truth is that neither that feeling in your throat, nor the one in your stomach, is responsible for your hunger or thirst.

Your blood should normally contain a certain amount of water and salt. This is also true of the tissues. Now, suppose this balance is upset for some reason. Your blood draws water from the tissues of your body in order to keep its balance constant. As this water is being removed, it registers in a "thirst center" in your brain. The thirst center sends an impulse to the pharynx, or throat, making it contract. This contraction makes you feel your throat is "dry," and you experience thirst.

The feeling of hunger originates in the brain, too. There is a hunger center that acts as a sort of brake on the activities of the stomach and intestines. When there is enough food in the blood, the hunger center slows up the action of the stomach and intestines. But if the blood doesn't have enough nourishment, the hunger center responds by releasing the brakes. The intestines become active, and we experience a feeling of hunger. Our stomach "growls."

To a certain degree we can control hunger by controlling the rate at which we use up our food supplies. In nature, the smaller and more active animals use up their food supply fastest. For example, a small bird may starve to death in five days, but it may take a dog twenty. When a person is calm, the protein stores of the body last longer than when he is excited or afraid.

There are people who can train themselves to go without food for long periods of time. They do this by a deliberate form of concentration, just as people can make themselves perform some exceptional athletic feat. It seems to be more difficult to control thirst, but people can make themselves able to endure it better by conscious efforts.

WHAT IS PROTEIN?

All living cells contain protein. This would suggest that protein is a substance necessary to life. And, in fact, we get our word "protein" from a Greek word meaning "first," because proteins are thought to be the most important part of living matter.

Each kind of cell has its own protein. The proteins are made up of combinations of substances called "amino acids." There are more than twenty-one different amino acids. Each amino acid group contains the chemical element nitrogen, in addition to carbon, hydrogen, and oxygen. The different amino acids can combine in different ways to form different proteins, and there are thousands of different proteins. For example, we all know that meat contains protein, but did you know that it is made up of at least twelve to fifteen different proteins?

Many of the foods that are considered important for us to eat are so because of the proteins they contain. These include milk, eggs, lean meats, fish, peas, beans, peanuts, and certain grains. They are important to man because they provide him with the amino acids that his body cannot make for itself. He must get the amino acids from the protein in the food he eats. In fact, they are called the "essential amino acids," which means the body cannot get along without them.

Certain kinds of amino acids, and definite amounts of them, are necessary so that the body tissues can use what they need. Plant proteins, such as those in peas, beans, and cereals, do not contain all the essential amino acids. But they are valuable in the diet when they are combined with some of the animal proteins.

Man cannot store amino acids in his body for later use. This means that the different kinds he needs have to be taken into the body at the same time. Bread and milk have to be eaten at the same meal, so the amino acids they provide can be used together to form new body tissue.

Moderate amounts of different kinds of protein foods should be eaten at each meal. In this way, you are sure of getting enough of the essential amino acids to meet the body's protein needs.

DO WE NEED TO TAKE EXTRA VITAMINS?

Vitamins are a group of substances found in food. The body needs them for life and health. So, naturally, a great many people are concerned with the question: Am I getting enough vitamins, and am I getting the right kind?

Even though very small amounts of each vitamin are enough for the needs of the body, the worry that people have about vitamins has some basis. And this has to do with their diet—the food they take in. A person eating a good variety of foods gets all the vitamins now known to be needed (with the possible exception of vitamin D).

The problem is that there are many people who don't choose foods wisely, don't get enough variety, and don't eat the basic foods they need to get their vitamins. So the answer to this question is: No, extra vitamins are not needed, providing you eat proper foods. In fact, many of the vitamins cannot be stored in the body, so when extra vitamins are taken in, the body simply gets rid of them.

It is even harmful to put too much of certain vitamins into the body. This has been found to be true of vitamins A and D, when large amounts are taken in capsules and liquids.

What foods supply what vitamins? Here is a quick, general idea. Vitamin A, for the health of the eyes, skin, teeth, and bones, is found in green, leafy vegetables, yellow vegetables, fruits, eggs, liver, and butter. B-1, which helps the nervous and digestive system and prevents certain diseases, is found in whole-grain bread, cereals, pork, and liver. B-2 is found in milk, eggs, greens, and lean meats.

Vitamin C, which helps tissues, bones, and teeth, is found in citrus fruits, tomatoes, and raw cabbage. Vitamin D is found in fortified milk and sunshine. These are only a few of the most important vitamins the body needs. The best thing to do is to get from your doctor a proper diet that includes the basic foods, and to be sure that you follow it.

WHAT IS PELLAGRA?

Pellagra is a disease that results when a person doesn't have enough of a certain vitamin. The vitamin is nicotinic acid, or niacin, which is one of the B-complex vitamins. Most persons with pellagra also suffer from deficiencies of riboflavin and other vitamins.

Pellagra occurs in most parts of the world, but it has been especially prevalent in the southeastern United States and in South Africa. The reason for this in the United States was that many people in this area lived chiefly on a diet of corn. With better diets and the addition of vitamins to many foods, pellagra has now become less common. Drug addiction and alcoholism can also lead to pellagra, because people who are addicted to alcohol or the use of drugs often fail to follow the proper diet and generally neglect their health and physical well-being.

Among the first symptoms of the disease are loss of appetite, loss of weight and strength, headache, and stomach upset. A person is also likely to get diarrhea and outbreaks of the skin.

The sores on the skin are deep-red areas that gradually turn brown and become large, thickened, and scaly. They are strongest about the neck and backs of hands and forearms. There is also an inflammation of the gums and lining of the stomach.

An even worse sign of this disease can be a kind of mental unbalance that takes the form of sleeplessness, depression, or even violent behavior. So you see, pellagra is a rather unpleasant disease. At one time, about 65 percent of all patients who had it died from it.

But when it was discovered that nicotinic acid could cure pellagra, the death rate dropped to a low level. Usually, the giving of this vitamin must be accompanied by other vitamins, too. And the person must go on a well-rounded diet.

Following this kind of treatment, the symptoms begin to disappear within a few hours, and a person can feel complete relief within a few days. In fact, even the most severe mental symptoms of this disease disappear quickly after treatment with nicotinic acid.

WHAT IS A GOITER?

In the front of your neck there is a very important gland of the body called the thyroid gland. It needs iodine in order to function.

While the body needs only a tiny amount of iodine, having this amount is essential. It helps in the formation of hormones, it is important in controlling the process of metabolism, and it has an effect on the nervous system.

The thyroid gland is subject to many different diseases, and the most common one is goiter. Goiter means an enlargement of the thyroid gland. The commonest form of goiter occurs in those parts of the world where the supply of iodine in the soil is low.

In mountainous areas, for example, iodine is often washed out of the soil, so the plants that grow there contain very little of it. Plant life is, directly or indirectly, the major source of food. So people in such areas soon become deficient in iodine.

What happens then is that the thyroid gland becomes enlarged in an effort to make up for the lack of iodine by producing more hormones. This enlarged gland is called a goiter. Sometimes such effort works, and sometimes not. It depends on the amount of iodine that reaches the thyroid. If there is no iodine at all reaching the body, then the enlargement of the gland doesn't solve the problem.

The amazing thing about this is the very tiny amount of iodine that is needed. The entire human body only contains about one fifteen-hundredth of an ounce of iodine. This is about two drops. And the daily requirement is even less, since iodine is used over and over again. By the way, this is why laws have been passed in many places requiring that iodine be added to table salt. Look at the box of salt in your home. It will probably have the word "Iodized" on it.

The addition of iodine to salt has done away with a good part of the goiter problem in the United States.

IS ALL HUMAN BLOOD THE SAME?

All human blood is made up of basically the same plasma, cells, and other chemical materials. But individuals differ in some of the arrangements and proportions of the chemicals in their cells and plasma.

There are four main groups, or types, of blood, and every human being can be classified under one of them. The groups are called A,B,O, and AB, based on the presence or absence of certain protein molecules in the blood.

When blood from two different groups is mixed and the blood

clumps, it is because of a reaction between the protein molecules in the red cells and the plasma. Such chemical reactions make it dangerous for a person to receive a transfusion of whole blood from someone whose blood group is unknown. But if the cells are removed from blood, then the remaining plasma can be given to anyone, no matter what his blood group.

Blood can be exchanged among human beings whose groups and subgroups have been matched. However, certain large populations may have more of one particular group than another. Anthropologists who study man's physical development use blood groups as one of the ways of showing relationships among individuals and population groups.

So although human blood has many different groups and subgroups, it is basically all the same. In fact, each species of animal has its own kind of blood. For example, all cats have the same kind of blood, just as all dogs have the same kind of blood. The blood of one species cannot be exchanged for the blood of another.

WHAT IS THE RH FACTOR?

When a person loses a great deal of blood for one reason or another, his life can often be saved by a blood transfusion. The blood of another person is put into the circulatory system and replaces his lost blood.

The first recorded blood transfusion was performed in 1677, when the blood of a lamb was injected into the veins of a dying boy. That boy was lucky and recovered. We now know that the blood of lower animals is different from human blood and cannot be used for transfusions with safety.

In 1940, it was found that there was still ancther way of dividing blood into groups, and this was according to the Rh factor. This discovery was made in the course of experiments on rhesus monkeys, and that's why it came to have the name "Rh."

It was found that when certain combinations of blood were made, the red blood cells broke apart. The cause was traced to certain differences in the Rh factor.

The blood of human beings in this case is divided into Rh positive and Rh negative. When blood from an Rh-positive person is transfused to a person who is Rh negative, the latter will develop a blood disease when he receives Rh-positive blood again.

In rare cases (one in forty or fifty), an Rh-positive father and Rh-negative mother will produce an infant with a blood disease if certain other conditions exist.

HOW DO BLOOD BANKS WORK?

Many hospitals have blood banks. In these banks, blood of all types is stored. When a unit of blood is needed, it is taken from the bank. Healthy people then give blood to the bank to replace the blood that is used. Blood can be kept refrigerated for about three weeks. A chemical such as sodium citrate is added to prevent clotting of the blood.

Transfusions are given mainly to replace blood that has been lost through severe bleeding. Such bleeding may occur as the result of illness, surgery, or accident.

Sometimes only a part of the blood is used for transfusions. Plasma, the liquid part of the blood, may be given alone. Transfusions of plasma are often given when people have been badly burned. In cases of severe burns, large amounts of plasma are lost from the bloodstream.

Transfusions of red blood cells alone may be used to treat certain cases of anemia. Anemia is a condition in which a person has too few red blood cells or his red blood cells contain too little hemoglobin.

When a person gets a transfusion, he gets blood of the same type as his. Otherwise there may be a bad reaction. For additional safety, the blood that is to be used in a transfusion is tested with the blood of the person who is to receive it. This testing is called cross matching of the blood.

Giving transfusions of blood that had been stored for some time was started by an American doctor, Oswald Robertson. He used it to treat wounded soldiers in 1918 in World War I.

WHAT IS HEMOPHILIA?

Did you know that you carry about an invisible first-aid kit in your blood? When a blood vessel is ruptured, nature applies "absorbent cotton" to stop the flow of blood. It isn't really absorbent cotton, of course, but it's something very much like it. It is a process known as clotting of the blood, and what makes it possible is the appearance of firm and very elastic fibrin threads that act as a sort of plug to stop the blood flow.

In every person's body the speed with which the blood clots form is different. There are some people whose blood clots very slowly or not at all. They are known as "bleeders," and their condition is called hemophilia.

Luckily, hemophilia is very rare. But, unfortunately, it is a condition that is inherited. It is transmitted in a peculiar way. Hemophilia appears only in men, but it is never transmitted directly from father to son.

It is transmitted from a father to a daughter, who herself remains healthy. She in turn gives it to her son, the grandchild of the sick father. So the rule for this disease goes like this: The son of a bleeder is always healthy and does not transmit the disease. The daughters of a bleeder are also healthy. Among their sons, however, the grandfather's disease reappears!

When the tragedy of this disease strikes it may be in a rich family or a poor one. In fact, this disease appeared in three of the most famous families in the world: in the Spanish royal family, in the Russian royal family, and in the children of Queen Victoria of England. In two of these cases, that of the Russian and the Spanish, the uncrowned successors to the throne were bleeders.

WHAT GIVES OUR EYES THEIR COLOR?

The eye is one of the most remarkable organs in our body. It is really a form of camera, with an adjustable opening to admit light, a lens that focuses the light waves to form an image, and a sensitive film on which the image is recorded.

Here we are not going to discuss "how we see," but rather the structure of the eye itself. The shape of the eye is round, except for a little bulge that sticks out in front where the light enters. This bulge, which curves outward in front, is called the cornea. The cornea is transparent. It helps bend the light rays as they enter the eye, and since it guards the opening into the eye, it is very sensitive. Any dust or dirt that alights on it is quickly felt so it can be removed.

The "camera film" of the eye is the retina. It is made up of ten very thin layers of cells and lines the entire inside of the eye. So now we have the opening to the eye, and the "film" which the light must reach inside.

To regulate the light coming in, we have the iris and the pupil of the eye. The iris is the circle of color, and the pupil is the little black dot in the center. By the way, the reason the pupil appears black is because it opens into the dark interior of the eye.

The size of the pupil is regulated by the iris, which closes the opening to a pinhole in bright light and expands the opening in dim light. Directly behind the iris and the pupil lies the lens, which is just like the lens of a magnifying glass. The lens is elastic and adjusts itself to long- or short-distance vision. It is the lens that bends the waves of light so that they will all come to a focus on the retina.

When we look into someone's eyes, the color we see is in the iris. The reason for this is that the fibers of the iris have pigments in them to protect the iris against light. The back part of the iris has most of the pigments, the front part almost none. Since the front part is very transparent and absorbs the red and yellow light waves as they pass through it, the light reflected from the pigmented part appears blue. The blue color is just a reflection of pigments from the back part of the iris.

If pigments don't develop in the front part of the iris in later years, the iris continues to look blue all through life. But if pigments do develop in the front of the iris, then it becomes brown.

WHY CAN'T WE SEE COLORS IN THE DARK?

Light from the sun or from any very hot source is called white light. But, as Newton was the first to show, white light is really a mixture of light of all colors.

When a beam of light is made to go through a glass prism, we see all the colors of the rainbow—red, orange, yellow, green, blue, and violet. Each shade blends gradually into the next without a break. This spread of color is called a spectrum.

These colors are present in sunlight to begin with, but show up only after being spread out by refraction in the prism. Each color is refracted a slightly different amount, red least and violet most. This spreading out is called dispersion. Without dispersion, the mixture gives the appearance of white to the eye.

Color is determined by the wavelength of the light (like the distance between one crest and the next in a wave traveling on water). The shortest visible light waves are violet; the longest are red.

Most of the colors we see in our surroundings are not of a single wavelength, but are mixtures of many wavelengths. When white light falls on an object, some wavelengths are reflected, and the rest are absorbed by the material. A piece of red cloth, for example, absorbs almost all wavelengths except a certain range of red ones. These are the only ones that are reflected to your eye, so you see the cloth as red.

So color is a quality of light. It does not exist apart from light. All our color sensations are caused by light rays entering our eyes. All objects are seen by reflected light, and the colors that they show exist in the light and not in the object.

DO DREAMS FORETELL THE FUTURE?

If we tried to assemble all the superstitious beliefs that have existed about dreams since the beginning of time, we could fill a library! Most of these superstitions have to do with the "meaning" of dreams, and the "meaning" usually has something to do with the future.

It isn't just primitive peoples who believed that dreams foretold the future. In Europe there were soothsayers who claimed they could read a person's future from his dreams. In fact, divining the future from dreams was a recognized art in ancient times and was called "oneiromancy." This is taken from the Greek word *oneiros,* which means "dream."

Of course, we are all familiar with the story in the Old Testament of how Joseph interpreted the Pharaoh's dreams. And we know that even today there are people who buy "dream books" that are supposed to help them foretell their futures from their dreams.

What does science today believe about the content of our dreams? Why do we dream what we dream, and what does it mean? For one thing, science does not accept the idea that dreams are a "message" to us from any source, foretelling the future.

The subject of our dreams comes from any of several sources. It may come from some stimulus that affects us at the very moment we are dreaming, such as a sound, or the fact that our feet are cold, or a breeze blowing over us.

The subject may also come from our store of past experiences, or something we are interested in, or some strong urge we feel. Sometimes in the dream we repeat past experiences almost exactly as they happened. At other times the events are rearranged in our dream. But the subject of our dream is a result of our past experience, and not a foreshadowing of the future.

WHAT CAUSES BLINDNESS?

Did you know that there are at least fourteen million blind people in the world? There are many degrees of blindness, so it is hard to define blindness. Some people cannot even see light. Others can only tell light from dark. Still others have a small amount of vision.

Of all the blind people in the world, only a small percentage were born blind. Blindness at birth is called congenital blindness. The causes of it are not all known.

Blindness that occurs after birth is caused mainly by diseases of the eyes. A general disease of the body, such as diabetes or meningitis, rather than a disease of the eye itself, may also cause blindness. Accidents and explosions are two other causes of blindness.

In countries where people live longer because of good medical care and a high standard of living, old age often brings on certain eye conditions. Two of these eye conditions are cataracts and glaucoma. Cataracts are the leading cause of blindness in the United States.

A cataract is a clouding of the lens of the eye. The lens, the transparent part of the eye through which light rays pass, becomes cloudy, and only strong light rays can pass through it. There is consequently a loss of vision. Cataracts can be removed by surgery.

With glaucoma, there is a hardening of the eyeball and great pressure inside the eye. Today there are medicines to control glaucoma if it is discovered in time.

The greatest single cause of loss of sight is trachoma. It is a contagious disease of the eyes caused by a virus. It affects the inner linings of the eyelids. Also, blood vessels grow over the cornea. This can destroy the vision.

Antibiotics can now control trachoma, but it is still common in some parts of Europe, Africa, and Asia.

WHAT IS CHICKEN POX?

The word "pox" means a disease with eruptions, and in chicken pox there are eruptions on the skin that may sometimes make it look like the skin of a chicken.

Chicken pox is also called "varicella," and is a contagious disease. While it is considered a childhood disease, adults may get it, too.

The specific organism that causes chicken pox has not yet been identified by medical science, but it is agreed that it is a virus. Chicken pox is passed on from one person to another by direct contact. It is rarely, if ever, passed on by contact with clothing or other articles touched by the infected person.

Here are the symptoms of chicken pox: a slight rise in temperature, loss of appetite, headache, and backache. Quite often, before any of these symptoms appear, a person breaks out in a rash or there are skin eruptions. The first skin eruptions are reddened spots about the size of a pinhead. They first show up in patches on the trunk of the body.

A few hours later, they enlarge and form blisters (vesicles) in the center of each spot. There is a clear fluid in the blister that later turns yellow, and then a crust or scab forms.

Most of the patches of eruptions appear on the back and chest. In severe cases almost all of the body may be covered.

Chicken pox is not considered a serious disease and usually requires little special treatment. But a doctor should be called to diagnose it and make sure there will be no complications.

The patient is usually made to stay in bed as long as new eruptions appear or there is some fever. Scratching the skin must be avoided to prevent infection or scars. One attack of chicken pox usually makes the person immune to the disease.

WHAT IS PLAGUE?

The first definite record we have of an outbreak of the plague is in the Old Testament. The Philistines were overcome by plague after they defeated the Israelites.

Plague is an acute infection that first attacks rats and other rodents, and then man. It is caused by an organism called *Bacillus pestis*. Fleas that live as parasites on the rodents transmit the disease by biting human beings.

When a person has plague, he has fever, chills, and swollen nodes in the groin. Spots also appear on the skin, and because these spots have a dark color, and because many people die of this disease, it was called the Black Death in the Middle Ages. It has also been called bubonic plague, and here is the reason: The swelling of nodes in the groin has been called a bubo, which comes from the Greek word *boubon,* meaning "groin." A serious epidemic of any kind is sometimes called a plague; but there is a definite disease called the plague.

One of the greatest outbreaks of the plague in history was the Black Death of the fourteenth century. It originated in Central Asia, reached the shores of the Black Sea, was brought into many European ports, and within five years had spread over the whole continent.

When plague appeared, the first reaction was usually panic, and people would try to leave the region. But not everyone could. All kinds of steps were taken to prevent the spread of the disease. People were isolated in their homes and couldn't leave, and no one could visit them. Food was provided by special messengers. When a plague patient died, everything he owned was burned.

Bubonic plague returned to Europe in the seventeenth century. Almost half the population of Lyons, France, died. Some eighty-six thousand people died in Milan, and almost five hundred thousand perished in the Venetian Republic.

Today all kinds of preventive measures are taken to stop the rise and spread of plague, and most of them deal with the control of rats.

CHAPTER 4
HOW OTHER CREATURES LIVE

WHAT IS THE WORLD'S LARGEST ANIMAL?

In prehistoric times there were gigantic creatures living on land and in the sea that were far larger than any animals alive today. The largest animal in existence today is the blue or sulphur-bottom whale. It may be over a hundred feet long and weigh 125 tons. And interestingly enough, about one-third of the length of this animal is taken up by its head!

Perhaps the most amazing thing about the whale is not its size, but the fact that it is a mammal and not a fish. Like all water mammals (such as dolphins and porpoises), whales are descended from ancestors that lived on land. There is evidence for this in the structure of their bodies. The skin and flesh of their paddlelike flippers cover the bones of a five-fingered "hand." Some whales even have the bones of hind legs embedded in their flesh.

Since the whale is a mammal, the baby whale is fed on its mother's milk like other little mammals. It is not hatched from an egg but is born alive, and for sometime after it is born it stays with its mother.

Whales have no gills, and breathe air through their lungs. They have horizontal tails, or flukes, which enable them to rise easily to the top of the water for air. The internal organs of the whale and the skeleton, circulatory system, and brain are also quite unlike those of the fish.

As whales developed and adapted themselves to life in the water, many changes took place; among them was the development of blubber. Mammals are warm-blooded animals, and it is very important for them to keep their body temperature within certain limits. Whales have a layer of fibrous tissue under their skin that is filled with oil and retains heat. On a larger whale, this layer of blubber may be from fourteen to twenty inches thick.

On the top of the whale's head are one or two blowholes; this makes it easier for them to breathe at the surface of the water. Underwater these nostrils are closed by little valves, and the air passages are shut off from the mouth, so there is no danger of taking water into the lungs. Whales can remain underwater for three-quarters of an hour!

WHAT IS A NARWHAL?

A narwhal is a type of whale, one of the most interesting of this fascinating family of creatures. Most of us think a whale is a whale, but there are actually quite a few varieties.

Toothed whales generally live on various types of fish that they chase and capture. Sperm whales are the largest of the toothed whales. They may be sixty-five feet long, and their heads are huge. Another toothed whale is the bottle-nosed whale, which has strange bony crests on either side of its head.

The narwhal is one of the toothed whales. It is found chiefly in Arctic waters and has something that cannot be found on any other whale: the male narwhal has a long ivory tusk on the left side of its mouth that sticks out in front like a sword!

WHAT ARE PINNIPEDS?

Pinnipeds are fin-footed mammals with limbs that they use as paddles or flippers. The three main kinds of pinnipeds are the walrus, the sea lion, and the seal.

They are all carnivores, or flesh eaters. They are aquatic (water) carnivores with the same distant ancestors as land carnivores such as dogs, cats, and bears.

These early ancestors lived on land many millions of years ago. Eventually one branch of these early carnivores took to the sea and became adapted to life in the water. These were the ancestors of our seal, sea lion, and walrus.

Today about thirty different kinds of pinnipeds live in the world's oceans. Most of them live in the cold waters of the Arctic and Antarctic oceans and in the nearby areas of the Atlantic and the Pacific. A few kinds range into warmer waters, and several forms live in freshwater lakes.

Since pinnipeds spend most of their lives in the water, they have become very well adapted for this kind of existence. All are expert swimmers. Their bodies are tapered and streamlined, with a thick layer of blubber that gives them added buoyancy in the water and helps them keep warm. The blubber also serves as a reserve of food when needed.

Pinnipeds are expert divers. They can go two hundred or three hundred feet down in search of food. Many of them have big eyes that are useful for seeing in the dim depths. When they are underwater, their nostrils close. Most of them have sharp, backward-pointing teeth, so that they can seize prey and direct it down the throat.

Pinnipeds are sociable animals and live together much of the time in large herds. This is especially true during the mating season or when pups are born. All of them must return to land, or at least be on a cake of ice, before bearing their young. The young seals, sea lions, and walruses are born with their eyes open and with full coats of hair or fur.

WHAT IS A SEA ELEPHANT?

The sea elephant might be considered a fourth kind of pinniped, but it is really a giant seal.

There are two species of the giant elephant seals, or sea elephants. One, the southern elephant seal, lives in waters around Antarctica. The other, the northern elephant seal, lives in waters off the coast of lower California, and breeds in Guadaloupe and other small islands.

Both species look very much alike and grow to about the same size. Big adult males may measure nearly twenty feet long and weigh up to eight thousand pounds! The females are much smaller, usually not more than nine or ten feet long. A single ninety to one hundred-pound pup is born about fifty weeks after the mating season.

The enormous male elephant seal has a long, dangling snout. When danger threatens, a male inflates his snout and roars loudly.

Because they were hunted for their hides and oil, the northern elephant seals were almost extinct by 1890. But the Mexican government stepped in and protected the herds, which slowly increased. Now, each year at the breeding grounds, as many as eight thousand to ten thousand of these huge creatures can be seen.

WHAT ARE OTTERS?

Otters belong to another group of animals, the mustelids. This word comes from the Latin, and means "weasel." Other members of this family of animals include weasels, skunks, and badgers. They are all short-legged, have thick coats of fur and sharp, tearing teeth, and are meat-eating mammals.

Otters love water, and their webbed feet, thick tails, and dense fur make them well suited for life in the water. Two kinds of otters are found in and around North America. One is a fresh-water otter; the other is a sea otter.

The fresh-water otter is found in streams and lakes from Mexico to Alaska. Its coat is a rich, dark brown. This otter is a restless animal, always on the move; a male sometimes wanders fifty or sixty miles during the winter. It is a very shy animal and is seldom seen by people.

The home of the fresh-water otter is usually a hole dug into the bank of a stream or lake. The hole leads to a den lined with leaves. Here the young, usually two or three to a litter, are born in late winter or early spring. Before the young can swim, the mother sometimes carries them about on her back in the water.

But the young learn very quickly to swim themselves. Their parents teach them to dive and to catch the fish on which they feed. Soon the cubs are able to stay underwater for as long as four minutes.

The sea otter is found off the western coast of North America, from California to Alaska, and in other northern waters. Sea otters are larger and heavier than fresh-water otters. Their thick fur is dark brown and has a frosted appearance. They have white whiskers from which they get the nickname, the "old men of the sea."

When they are not in a hurry, sea otters often swim and float on their backs. They use their stomachs as tables from which they eat crabs, sea urchins, mollusks, and other sea creatures.

Sea otters were widely hunted for their valuable fur, and they almost became extinct. But they are now protected by international treaty and are coming back in great numbers.

WHAT IS A NEWT?

Newts are a certain kind of salamander. They belong to the class of animals known as amphibians, which includes frogs and toads as well as salamanders. Most amphibians spend part of their lives in water and part on land.

Today there are only three main groups of amphibians: frogs and toads, which have no tails as adults; salamanders and newts, which do have tails; and caecilians, which have tails but no legs.

Because newts have long bodies, people sometimes mistake them for lizards. But there is a way to tell them from lizards: lizards have scales, salamanders do not; lizards have claws, and salamanders do not.

Newts like to keep their bodies cool. Most of them live in the temperate zones of North America and Europe, where the winters are cold. Here they have adapted in various ways to the world around them. They may live entirely in the water or in underground caves. They may live in rotting trees or in cracks in rocks. On land they crawl or walk on small, weak legs. In water a salamander or newt swims or wriggles, helped by its long tail.

Newts are usually smaller than most other salamanders and have a thicker, drier skin. They are found in Asia, North Africa, Europe, and North America.

One kind of newt common in the United States leads a triple life. The eastern or red-spotted newt starts life in the water. In two or three months the tiny, light-green tadpole completes its metamorphosis and is ready for life on land. The newt turns coral-red, with two rows of black-bordered red spots on its back. It is now about one-and-a-half to three inches long, and is called the red eft.

After two or three years on land, the eft returns to water to lay its eggs. Its skin changes again, turning olive green on top. The skin becomes smooth. The round tail grows new fins. And the newt lives the third stage of its life in the water.

WHAT ARE LIZARDS?

Lizards are reptiles, a class of animals that also includes crocodiles, turtles, and snakes. There are about three thousand kinds of lizards.

A typical lizard is four-legged, short-bodied, and long-tailed. All lizards shed their scaly skins. They may do this several times a year. Lizards are found in all parts of the world except the polar regions. They thrive in tropical regions, but are also found in the temperate regions. Lizards of the temperate regions must hibernate in the winter.

Most lizards are small, usually less than two feet in length. The largest lizards are the Komodo monitors of Indonesia, which may grow to ten feet in length and weigh three hundred pounds. A lizard like that looks pretty much like the dragons of fairy tales.

As a rule, lizards have short life spans. Some live only two or three years. The record for a lizard in captivity is about twenty-five years.

Most lizards eat insects that they catch with their tongues or snap out of the air. They usually eat food that can be swallowed whole. Lizards have teeth that help hold their food, but they rarely use these teeth to bite off food.

Some lizards have quite specialized diets. The horned lizard usually eats only ants. Other lizards eat plants or perhaps only fruit. The large monitor lizard is one of the few meat-eating lizards. It eats dead animals and sometimes catches small wild pigs, which it swallows whole.

Most kinds of lizards are hatched from eggs, although many are born alive. The eggs are buried in the soil or hidden in decaying logs. Often the female guards the eggs against animals that might feed on them. The young have a special "egg tooth" that grows up from the tip of the upper jaw. The tooth is used to cut through the eggshell at the time of hatching, and then the tooth disappears.

Many lizards live in deserts. They can withstand the heat and dryness that make it impossible for most other animals to stay alive there.

WHAT IS A HORSESHOE CRAB?

A horseshoe crab is a rather fascinating creature. To begin with, it isn't a crab, and it doesn't look much like a horseshoe. It is, however, related to crabs and spiders.

Its scientific name, *Limulus polyphemus,* describes its eyes. The animal has four eyes. One pair bulges from the sides; the other two are set close together at the front of the head and look like one eye.

A horseshoe crab is what scientists call a living fossil. Its body form has changed very little during millions of years. In fact, it has existed in its present form for almost 200 million years!

The entire body is armored by a thick shell. The tail is sword-shaped, long and pointed. It is also barbed. If the horseshoe crab is overturned by a wave, it uses the tail to right itself.

A horseshoe crab has six pairs of legs. Four pairs are used for walking along the sandy bottom of the ocean. A stronger back pair is used in pushing and swimming. A short front pair helps hold and push food toward the mouth. This mouth is practically hidden by the walking legs, so it's hard to find when you look for it.

The "shoulders," or inner joints, bear spikes. These grind and tear food and stuff it into the mouth. A horseshoe crab eats almost anything, from small clams, worms, and fish eggs to seaweed and decaying matter.

A horseshoe crab breathes by means of gill books. Each gill book has about 150 thin leaves, which take oxygen from the water. As long as these leaves stay moist, the animal can breathe.

Baby horseshoe crabs hatch from very tiny eggs. They are born without a tail and with a very soft shell. In about four weeks it is too large for its shell. The shell does not grow, so the animal must shed its shell, or molt.

Before a horseshoe crab reaches its full length of one to two feet, it may molt as many as twenty times!

WHAT IS THE DIFFERENCE BETWEEN OYSTERS AND CLAMS?

There is a large group of animals that scientists call mollusks. The name comes from a Latin word meaning "soft." All mollusks are alike in that they have soft bodies that are covered by a thin envelope of flesh. The envelope is called a mantle. Oysters and clams belong to the mollusk family of animals.

Some mollusks have two shells. They are called bivalves (meaning "two shells"). Oysters, mussels, clams, and scallops are bivalves.

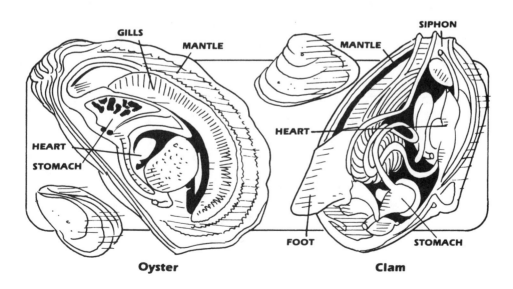

Oyster   Clam

Oysters generally live in shallow waters, where they may be found cemented to rocks and shells near river mouths or along shores. The shells of an oyster open a little when it is feeding and close tightly when it is disturbed. An oyster withdraws into its shell when an enemy approaches or when the tide goes down.

The main body parts of an oyster—including heart, stomach, kidneys, and gills—lie inside the mantle. An oyster has no head, but it does have a mouth. It feeds by straining food out of the water. Food particles are drawn into a space between the soft body and the mantle. They stick to mucus that is produced by the gills. Then the food is passed along from the gills to the mouth folds and, finally, into the mouth.

Clams are usually found buried in sand or mud anywhere from just below the level of low tide out to depths of several hundred feet. Clams burrow into the sand or mud to protect themselves from various enemies and to secure firm anchorage.

A clam has a large foot that it uses for burrowing and for withdrawing quickly into the sand. When the clam wants to move from place to place, the first thing it does is extend this foot. There is a cavity in the foot, and when the clam extends it, blood rushes into the cavity. This makes the tip of the foot swell up, and it provides a kind of anchor. Then the clam contracts the muscles in the foot. Since the foot is anchored, it stays in place, and the clam's body moves forward. The clam's tough shell prevents sand or mud from pressing in on the soft body and smothering it.

No matter how deep a clam may be in the sand or mud, it gets food and oxygen from the water. It can do this because its mantle has a necklike portion that can stretch upward to the surface of the sand. This neck is called a siphon. It has two tubes. Through one tube, water is sucked in, and food and oxygen dissolved in the water are used by the animal. Water passes out again through the second tube.

HOW DO OYSTERS EAT?

When you examine an oyster in its shell you can easily wonder how it does anything but just lie there! How does it breathe, eat, protect itself?

The oyster, however, is not just a glob of living matter; it is quite a complicated creature that carries on many complex activities. It has various organs, blood, a nervous system, and so on. But here we will only concern ourselves with how the oyster eats.

First of all, what does it eat? The food of an oyster consists of tiny algae and other micro-organisms. This means organisms so small that they can only be seen under a microscope. These tiny food particles enter into the body of the oyster with the water that constantly "flows" through the oyster when its shell is open.

The food is strained from the water and becomes entangled in the mucus secreted by the gills of the oyster. The oyster actually selects certain food and rejects other organisms that are unsuitable or too big or the wrong shape, but we don't know how it is able to do this.

The oyster has an alimentary canal that begins at its mouth, and four feelers that guard the mouth's opening. These feelers receive and sort out the food.

There is a narrow esophagus that opens into the stomach, which is a large, saclike structure. A sort of rod about half an inch long projects into the stomach. This rod rotates in the stomach, mixing and grinding the small food particles. This rod also contains the enzymes that digest the food. There is also a large digestive gland surrounding the stomach.

In this gland there are blood cells that surround the food and digest it inside their bodies. Of course, this is only a rough idea of the whole eating process—but you can see that an oyster does eat!

HOW DOES A SPONGE EAT?

It may seem hard to believe, but sponges are animals! They are among the strangest members of the animal kingdom, and they look much more like plants than animals.

There are more than five thousand different kinds of sponges. They range in color from green, brown, yellow, red, and orange to white. They may be shaped like fans, domes, vases, bowls, or trumpets.

Some sponges branch out like trees. Others are flattened masses of spongy tissue spread out on the surface of underwater rocks, shells, or wood. Some are small, less than an inch long. Others are big, measuring two or three feet in height or width.

Adult sponges never move about. And even though a sponge is a living animal, when you touch one it doesn't react. A sponge does not have a head or mouth. It has no eyes, ears, feelers, or other sense organs. And a sponge has no heart, stomach, muscles, or nervous system. If a living sponge is cut in two, all you see is a slimy mass with holes or channels running through it.

This doesn't make it seem much like an animal, does it? And you can understand why even scientists didn't realize for a long time that sponges actually were animals.

Then what does make a sponge an animal?—The way it feeds, chiefly. A sponge captures its food. It does not make its own food, as green plants do. It captures tiny plants and animals from the water around it.

How does it do this? The tube wall of a sponge is like a sieve, or filter, that strains tiny plants and animals out of the water. Water is forced in and out of the sponge by the beating action of tiny, whip-like threads (called flagella). The cells with flagella capture the food. Around the bottom of the flagella, there is a sticky surface that catches the food. Some of the food is digested there and some is passed on to the rest of the sponge by cells that wander through the sponge.

WHAT DO TURTLES EAT?

Turtles have many very interesting and unusual attributes, but their food habits are rather ordinary. The fact is, most turtles eat just about anything.

It depends, of course, on the particular kind of turtle. The snapping turtle, which is not a very pleasant creature to meet, is quite a good hunter. It feeds under water chiefly on fish, frogs, and even ducks!

The terrapin turtle, which people themselves like to eat, can eat its food best under water. It eats insects, tadpoles, and fish. The box turtle, which is a sort of connecting link between the land and the water turtles, likes to spend most of its time on land. But in the hot summer months it enjoys cooling off in the water. When it is on land, it likes to wander through the woods in search of berries and fungi.

Gopher turtles dig burrows in dry, barren places in which they rest during the day. In the early evening they come out and search for their favorite foods—fruit and vegetation.

And what do turtles do in the winter, when their food supply disappears? Like all reptiles, turtles who live in temperate climates go to sleep during the winter months. The length of their sleep depends on the climate. But many turtles can go without food and sleep away the time from October until March! Turtles that live in the water usually bury themselves in the bottoms of rivers and ponds. Land turtles hide themselves in the ground to spend the winter.

Land turtles breathe air through lungs, and have shells made up of a "bony box" covered with horny plates or with soft skin. These shells are divided into two parts. One part covers the back; the other covers the underpart of the turtle's body. Through the openings between the two parts the turtle can thrust out its head, neck, tail, and legs.

Turtles have a good sense of sight, taste, and touch, but their hearing is poorly developed.

HOW DO FROGS CROAK?

If you've ever lived near a pond, then you were sure to wonder about the croaking of frogs. The noises they sometimes make at night can be enough to keep you from sleeping!

While some female frogs may make certain sounds when they are injured, the familiar singing or croaking we hear is limited to the male. The chief reason he sings his throaty song is to attract the female. But he doesn't limit his croaking to the mating season. His voice can be heard at night long after the mating season is past.

This is the way a frog makes that croaking sound. He inhales, closes his nostrils and mouth, and forces the air back and forth between the mouth and lungs. The sound is produced when the air passes over the vocal cords and causes them to vibrate.

Many kinds of frogs have vocal sacs that open into the mouth. When the frog is singing, these sacs become filled with air and enlarge. These enlarged sacs act as resonators and help give the frog's croaking that peculiar sound. By the way, the American bullfrog's voice may sometimes be heard from a distance of a mile or more!

While the adult frog has lungs, it does not breathe air into them as we do. It sucks air into its mouth through two nostrils, at the same time lowering its throat. Then the nostrils are closed, and the frog lifts its throat and pushes the air into its lungs.

Did you know that the frog uses its eyes in swallowing food? As you know, frogs catch their prey with sticky tongues. When an insect sticks to the tongue, it is folded back into the mouth. The large, bulging eyes of the frog are separated from the mouth cavity by only a thin skin. When closed, they bulge inward. So the frog closes its eyes when it has an insect in its mouth, and the inner bulging helps to push the food down its throat! Frogs are useful to man because they are insect eaters and help keep the insect population down.

HOW MANY KINDS OF INSECTS ARE THERE?

What do most people think of when you mention "insects"? Well, they may think of pests, such as flies, mosquitos, moths, and beetles.

Or, they may think of ants and bees and wasps; and attractive insects like butterflies. And then if you ask if they can think of any more insects, they might be able to think of a few more.

But do you know how many different kinds of insects there actually are? Get ready for a surprise. There are somewhere between two and four million different kinds of insects! Scientists have actually described in scientific language as many as 625,000 different kinds. They practically have no hope of ever being able to classify every single kind of insect that exists. There is no other class of animals on earth that even comes close to having as many kinds as do insects.

When it comes to trying to estimate how many insects are living in the world today, the number is so vast that the human mind cannot even imagine it! The only way scientists can even begin to count the insect population in any one area is to count all the insects that can be found in and on a square yard of rich, moist soil. That can be anywhere from five hundred to two thousand. So it can be said that in a single acre of good soil, about four million insects live in cozy comfort!

Remember that if you, who are untrained in observing insects, were to go over this same acre and count insects, you would see only an occasional butterfly, bumblebee, or beetle. But the majority of insects are so small that the human eye does not readily notice them. Many are microscopic. And there are only a few thousand insects of all those that exist that become annoying enough to man for him to try to control them.

When you think of it this way, you realize that man really moves about in a world of insects—but he has no idea that most of them exist or how many there are!

By the way, there are two things most insects have in common: Their body is divided into three parts; and they usually have six legs. This is true of most, but not all of them.

WHAT ARE FLEAS?

Most of us think of fleas as the tiny creatures that live on dogs and cause them to be constantly scratching. But did you know that there are more than nine hundred different species of fleas?

Fleas are parasitic insects, which means they live on other creatures. They live on all mammals (including man), as well as on birds and many other animals. In fact, next to flies, fleas are the insects with which people all over the world are most familiar. This is because they infect domestic animals and man, and have done so since the earliest times.

The bite of a flea can cause quite a bit of discomfort, but that is not the chief reason they are troublesome. Fleas can carry serious diseases, like typhus fever and bubonic plague, which may result in death.

Fleas lay their tiny eggs right on the host animal on whom they are living, or in the places where the host sleeps. The eggs are scattered widely by the movement of the host.

Larvae come out of the eggs, and when these are mature, they spin a tiny cocoon, and out of this the adult flea eventually comes. It only takes twenty-eight to forty-eight days for the human flea to develop from an egg stage to an adult. The rat flea in the tropics takes only twenty-one days.

An adult flea has no wings. But it has well-developed legs that it uses for leaping, and some species of fleas are quite remarkable leapers. Some can jump as high as eight inches straight up and thirteen inches horizontally!

The mouth parts of a flea are adapted to pierce the skin of other animals and to suck blood, on which they live. The body itself is flat.

Fleas are most abundant in the tropics and warmer regions, but they also exist in the polar regions and in deserts. In North America, the most important species of fleas are the human flea, the dog flea, and the cat flea. All three kinds, however, attack humans, dogs, and cats, among other animals.

DO ANTS HAVE A SENSE OF SMELL?

Ants are such amazing insects that it would take much more space than we have here to tell their fascinating story. So let's just consider a few facts about them for now.

To begin with, you'll find ants in desert sands, prairies, seashores, mountain slopes, forests—practically anywhere in the world, except perhaps on the very summit of the highest mountains! They can endure almost all kinds of climates.

There are thousands of different species of ants, but they all are related to bees and wasps; that is, they belong to the same order of insects. All ants are social. This means that ants live in colonies. Each colony has three sorts of ants: the males; the females, or queens; and the workers.

The males and the queens of most species of ants have wings, but the workers are wingless. The queen gets rid of her wings after her mating flight. The colonies of ants vary greatly in size. Some may have only a few dozen ants living together; others may have hundreds of thousands of busy ants in the same colony!

Although ants vary greatly in size, they are all more or less alike in appearance. A pair of long feelers, or antennae, wave from the ant's head. These are constantly moving, and they serve not only as feelers, but also as organs of smell. So while the ant doesn't have a "nose" for smelling, it does have a sense of smell. The antennae also help the ant to distinguish other ants and to communicate with them.

The head of the ant also contains the brain, a pair of compound eyes, and its powerful jaws and mouth. In addition to the compound eyes, most ants have other seeing organs called simple eyes, or stemmata.

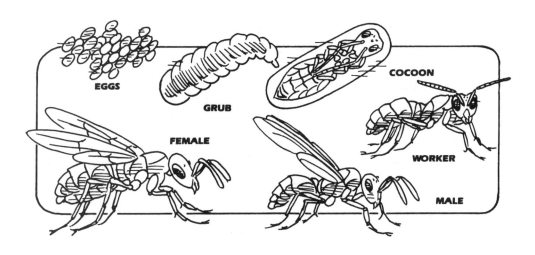

The life cycle of the ant is a fascinating one. The females of a colony fly high into the air, and the males follow them. After this mating flight, the males die almost at once, and each female, or queen, goes off by herself and starts a new colony. She digs a nest and lays some eggs. After these eggs hatch into little legless grubs, the queen mother helps each spin a cocoon. When the young ant has grown, she cracks open one end of the cocoon and pulls the ant out of its shell. Almost at once, these newborn worker ants begin their life of devotion to their mother and to the rest of the colony.

WHAT IS AN ANTEATER?

The anteater is an animal that feeds on white ants, the kind of ants we usually call termites. The anteater probably chooses ants rather than other foods because it has no teeth. Its very long jawbone is almost entirely covered with skin.

The anteater has a very small mouth and a wormlike tongue that is more than a foot long and is covered with a sticky substance. When the anteater sees a termite, it pushes out its tongue. The termite is trapped on the sticky substance until the anteater swallows down its prey.

Because many of the termites that the anteater hunts build large nests of hard mud, Nature has given it powerful forearms and long claws. The anteater uses its long claws to tear open the termite nest.

There are three kinds of anteaters, and each is quite different from the other. The giant anteater lives on the ground. It is about seven feet long; its head takes up about a foot of this length and its tail measures two feet. It has long, coarse hair. The claws on the front feet are so long that the anteater can't walk on them. It has to move along on the sides of its feet instead of the soles. The giant anteater feeds at night and sleeps all day.

The tamandua is another kind of anteater. It is about three feet long and has short hair. The tamandua uses its tail for many things. Without its tail, the tamandua would not be able to live in trees as it does.

The silky anteater is the smallest anteater of all. It is about a foot and a half long, half of which is the tail. So it can also live in trees. In fact, it spends the day curled up on a branch. The silky anteater lives in the area between southern Mexico and Brazil.

WHAT DO MOTHS EAT?

Most of us worry about moths in terms of destruction to our clothes. While clothes moths—in their caterpillar stage—do eat articles made from wool, fur, and other animal matter, they are not the only destructive moths in existence. Let's just go down the list of some other moths and see what they eat, or destroy.

The clearwing moth eats woody plants. There are peach, currant, and squash borers and you can guess their favorite foods. Then there is a species of moth that eats grain and potatoes. The pink bollworm, a very destructive type, eats cotton.

There are also pea moths, strawberry leaf folder moths, grapeberry moths, and bud moths. The species known as Pyralidae includes eight families of moths, all of them very destructive, including the European corn borer, the melon worm, the celery leaf tier, the meal moth (which feeds on cereals and other seeds), the oriental rice borer, and the sugarcane borer.

The larvae of the wax moth feed on wax, even going into beehives where they often cause serious damage. The Indian-meal moth is one of the worst destroyers of such foods as cereals, flour, nuts, and dried fruits.

Many of the tiger moths eat cultivated crops and trees. Some hawk moths feed on tobacco, tomatoes, grapes, and apples. The coddling moth is the chief pest in the apple orchard.

But, remember, adult moths eat only nectar from flowers. It is when the moth is in the caterpillar stage that it eats all these other things.

By the way, the caterpillars of some moths have actually been used as food by some primitive peoples. For example, Indians in certain parts of the western United States ate the caterpillars of the Coloradia pandora moth.

DO INSECTS HAVE BLOOD?

As we look at living creatures much smaller than ourselves, many of us imagine that they must lack the organs and functions that we have. How can something as tiny as an insect have a heart? How can it have a circulatory system and blood in its tiny body?

But the miracle of life is not only that these creatures have organs, but that these organs are perfect for each insect's way of life.

Adult insects have bodies with three sections: head, thorax, and abdomen. The head has a pair of antennae in front that are feelers, and that usually have some tiny organs of smell. The eyes and mouth are part of the head, too.

Not only does an insect have a heart, but it also has blood and a circulatory system. The blood passes into the heart by means of holes equipped with valves. When the heart contracts, these holes close, and the blood is driven out through the arteries. Insects don't have a system of capillaries and veins as we do.

The reason their circulatory system is not greatly developed is that they don't depend on the circulation of the blood for their supply of oxygen. In our bodies, as you know, the blood carries oxygen to every part and enables it to function.

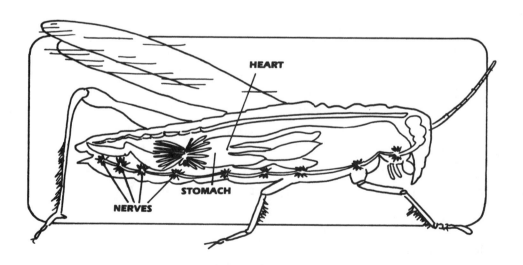

But insects have a different system of breathing. They have tiny branching tubes that end in little air holes in the sides of the body. The air comes in right from the surface of the body and goes directly to the cells.

A more complicated system would be too much for their size. On the other hand, a simple system like theirs wouldn't be enough for larger animals. It's not too bad a system, though, considering that more than half of all living animals have it!

Did you know that one name for an insect is hexapod? The term is from two Greek words meaning "six" and "foot." If you count the feet of an insect, you can see why hexapod is a good way to describe most insects. The legs are usually in three pairs, and are attached to the thorax.

There are thousands and thousands of different species of insects, among them some of man's best friends as well as some of his worst enemies.

WHERE DO SNAKES GET THEIR VENOM?

Scientists think there are about two thousand four hundred different kinds of snakes now living. Of these, only about 8 percent are poisonous kinds that stun or kill their prey with venom. In many poisonous snakes the venom is not strong enough or plentiful enough to be dangerous to man.

All snakes have a large amount of saliva that helps them swallow and digest prey. In the venomous snakes one of the saliva glands produces a substance that is poisonous to the snakes' prey. This substance is the snakes' venom.

Some snakes have venom that is strong enough to kill an elephant. Others have venom so mild that they can kill only small lizards. Probably only two hundred species of venomous snakes can be considered dangerous to man.

Among the venomous species of snakes known, the cobras and their relatives make up one family; the vipers, a second. And there are some venomous snakes among a kind known as the colubrids, the largest family of snakes.

The cobras and their relatives have fangs at the front of the mouth, one on each side of the upper jaw. The fangs are grooved, but in most cobras the groove is closed over, forming a hollow tube. A muscle surrounds the venom gland. When the snake bites, the muscle presses on the gland. This forces the venom down into the fang and out through the fang tip directly into the prey.

There is a spitting cobra that can spray venom from its fangs. The cobra aims at the eyes of a threatening animal, such as an antelope or buffalo. The spray reaches about eight feet and causes almost instant blindness.

In general, cobra venom affects the nervous system of the victim and makes him unable to move. When the venom reaches the nerve centers that control breathing or heartbeat, the victim dies.

Vipers have very long fangs. Their venom affects mainly the blood cells and blood vessels of the victims. It may cause great swelling and bleeding.

WHAT DO SNAKES EAT?

There are no "vegetarian" snakes. They are all carnivores and eat animals of some kind.

Snakes have powerful digestive juices—and they need them, for snakes always eat their meal whole. They do not have teeth that can cut up food, such as cats have, for example. Birds and turtles have sharp beaks. All that snakes have are slender, needlelike teeth with which they can catch their prey and pull it into their mouth. But they can't chew it up.

One of the most unusual things about snakes and their eating is the construction of their jaws. The jaws are very loosely attached to the other bones of the skull. They are edged with teeth, and most snakes also have two rows of teeth in the roof of the mouth. All these rows of teeth are on bones moved by special muscles.

A snake eats by pushing one jaw over the food while the teeth of the rest of the jaw hold the prey. Then another jawbone is pushed over the food. In this way the food is pulled down into the throat of the snake.

Because of the arrangement of the jaws, a snake can eat animals that are surprisingly big. For example, pythons sometimes eat animals that are as large as deer and leopards! Of course, small snakes eat small animals. Most snakes eat animals of moderate size: grasshoppers, frogs, fish, mice, rats, and birds. Some tiny blind snakes eat only termites. And there are some snakes that eat other snakes!

Snakes tend to be particular about what they eat. A green snake may eat spiders, fish, birds and caterpillars, but not lizards or mice. And a water snake may eat fish and frogs, but not insects or mice. Garter snakes, however, seem able to eat a variety of animals, including worms, fish, frogs, rodents, and birds.

HOW DO WOLVES HUNT?

The wolf has always had a bad reputation. It is cast as the villain of many of Aesop's fables and countless nursery rhymes and fairy tales. Little Red Riding Hood was pursued by a greedy wolf, and so were the three little pigs.

How does this creature go about getting its food? When searching for food, wolves travel regular hunting trails that may extend for a hundred miles or more. Sometimes several weeks pass before the wolves cover the entire circuit. From time to time the wolves fan out—eyes, ears, and noses alert for possible prey.

At intervals along the trail, the wolves have "scent posts." These are stumps, trees, rocks, or other landmarks upon which they urinate, just as dogs do on fireplugs or shrubbery. Each time a wolf comes to a scent post, he sniffs it carefully. In this way he learns what other wolves have passed that way.

The main food of wolves is meat, and the kind depends on what prey is most readily available. Wolves will attack and eat deer, moose, and many other large, hoofed animals. In Canada and Alaska, wolves follow herds of caribou and prey on the calves and stragglers.

In the Arctic, they sometimes attack musk oxen. And whenever domestic stock is left unguarded in wild country, it is likely to be killed and eaten. Rabbits and rodents are hunted when no easier prey is around. If wolves can't find any meat, they will eat fruit, such as berries.

Sometimes wolves track their prey for many hours. They keep up a tireless pace that is not swift, but that they can continue for mile after mile. Finally the prey is brought to bay. Several wolves may attack from the rear, others from the front. When the quarry finally goes down, the pack swarms all over it, slashing and biting until the victim is dead.

Then all the members of the pack gorge themselves, sometimes eating as much as fifteen pounds of meat each. The remainder of the meat may be hidden or buried as a supply for future meals.

HOW DO ELEPHANTS LIVE IN HERDS?

An elephant herd may vary from ten or twenty animals to fifty or more, most of whom are related.

The leader of the herd is usually a wise old cow, or female elephant. Most of her followers are females with young in various stages of growth. Young males also travel with the herd, but adult bulls often travel alone. Many live apart from the herd, but visit it often.

When two or more bulls join the herd at the same time, they are likely to fight each other. When one of them gains the upper hand, he may gore the other, drive him away, or even kill him.

The herd wanders far and wide, visiting favorite food areas at different times of the year. During the dry season they migrate into forests or stay close to a good supply of water. In the rainy season they wander out onto grassy plains.

The daily life of an elephant herd often follows a routine. In the early morning hours the animals may travel to a nearby river. There they drink and bathe—snorting and rolling and squirting water over themselves. Elephants are good swimmers and can cross broad rivers.

After bathing, the elephants feed on trees and other plants for several hours. Then they pause in some shady area for a midday rest. As evening comes on they sometimes go back to the river to drink again.

They may feed far into the night before taking another rest period. Some elephants lie down to sleep, but many adults—especially among the African elephants—sleep standing up.

All the adult elephants in a herd are constantly on the alert for danger. They have poor eyesight and only fair hearing, but they have a keen sense of smell. When a youngster in a herd is attacked—possibly by a lion or tiger—the rest of the herd rallies to its defense. In Asia, tigers kill about one of every four elephant calves. Adult elephants are rarely attacked by any other animal.

WHAT IS A GAZELLE?

A gazelle is a kind of antelope. There are about a hundred species of antelopes, which are members of the cattle family and which are characterized by their graceful build and upward-sweeping horns.

The graceful horns of some gazelles look like a lyre. These horns may be heavy, streamlined, or bent, varying in shape from a V or U to a bracket, depending on the species.

A gazelle is about twenty-six inches high.

The expression "swift as a gazelle" comes from the fact that they can move with great speed. A gazelle can run faster than a greyhound.

Antelopes as a whole are most abundant in Africa, where there are about ninety species. Ten species are found in India. At one time antelopes lived over most of Europe and Asia.

All male antelopes have horns, and in half the species, females have horns, too. Some kinds have only one-inch spikes, while the giant sable antelope has tremendous sixty-four-inch half-circles.

Most antelopes are graceful and shy, but certain species, such as the wildebeest, sable, roan, eland, and oryx, are dangerous when approached or wounded. The wildebeest, or gnu, looks like a horse with a beard and buffalo horns, and is especially savage. It has such great endurance and speed that it can easily outdistance a horse.

Many antelopes live on open plains, often in herds of hundreds. Others live singly or in small herds. Some live in marshes, near riverbanks, on cliffs, or in deserts.

Antelopes are usually tawny, reddish, or gray, often with white belly, rump, and face markings. Some are beautifully marked and colored. Antelopes walk on two-toed hoofs and, like other cattle, ruminate, or chew the cud.

IS THE DUCKBILL A MAMMAL OR A BIRD?

It would be hard to find a stranger creature in all the world than the duckbill, or platypus. The chances are that you will never see a live duckbill, because it dies in captivity. What makes this creature so odd?

For one thing, the duckbill is like a fish, like a fowl, and like a reptile, yet it is not any of them! It's a kind of in-between animal that came about by evolution.

Mammals nurse their young, and so does the duckbill. Fowl and birds lay eggs, and so does the duckbill. The body temperature of a reptile changes with the heat or cold of its surroundings, and this also happens to the duckbill! Actually, however, the duckbill is a mammal, one of the only two mammals that lay eggs (the other is the anteater).

The duckbill has webbed feet and a ducklike bill instead of a mouth. It swims in the water somewhat like a fish. It is found only in the eastern portion of Australia and in Tasmania.

The males are about twenty-one inches long, and the females, about eighteen inches. The body is covered with a fine underfur hidden by a coat of long, coarse guard hairs, whose ends turn in toward the body. It has a flat tail, somewhat like a beaver's. The duckbill can hear quite well, even though it looks as if it has no ears. It hears with a set of internal ears.

The duckbill can't breathe underwater, so it must keep its bill in the air while it swims. But since the nostrils are about one-third of the distance from the tip of the bill, it has to keep only the end of its bill out of water.

On the heel of each hind foot of the male is a horny organ connected with poison glands, so this creature can take pretty good care of itself. This peculiar animal makes its home in burrows in the banks of quiet, deep pools in rivers. The duckbills stay in the burrow most of the day and come out only at night to feed in the water. They eat water insects, worms, and shellfish.

The duckbill builds a special burrow for nesting purposes, which it fills with leaves, grass, and reeds. The female lays her eggs in the nest and lies curled around them to incubate them. The young are born blind and helpless, and remain in the burrow for some time, feeding upon the mother's milk.

WHAT IS THE BALD EAGLE?

The bald eagle is an American bird. Despite its name, it is not what we think of as bald.

The bald eagle was named at a time when "bald" meant "white" or "streaked with white." The adult bald eagle has white feathers on its head. Its tail is white, too. Its body and wings are dark brown, and its eyes, beak, and feet are yellow.

The bald eagle is fond of fish and likes to live near water. It feeds mainly on dead or dying fish. Sometimes the eagle steals its catch from the osprey, another large fishing bird. The bald eagle also eats small animals, such as rabbits or birds.

The bald eagle is the national emblem of the United States. Like all the other eagles in North America, it is becoming rare. But eagles are among the most interesting birds known to man.

Some eagles are more than three feet long from head to tail, and their wingspread may be more than seven feet. An eagle's beak is large and hooked. Its toes end in talons, which are strong claws. An eagle has far keener eyesight than a human being.

An eagle is a bird of prey; that is, a hunter. The eagle swoops down, picks up the prey in its talons, and flies off. An eagle, which weighs eight to twelve pounds, may be able to carry off an animal weighing as much as seven-and-one-half pounds! With its beak, it tears the food to pieces. Eagles, by the way, hunt only in the daytime.

An eagle keeps the same mate for many years, perhaps for life —no one is sure. A pair of eagles build their nest at the top of a very tall tree or on a rocky ledge. The nest, called an aerie, is built of sticks. The largest aerie on record is nine-and-one-half feet wide and twenty feet deep. Many eagles use the same nests year after year. An eagle may live as long as thirty years.

DO ANY BIRDS HIBERNATE?

When the cold of winter comes, we can tuck ourselves into a warm house, sit by the fire, and stay indoors until we want to go out. But even though we are a warm-blooded animal, we can't hibernate. If man did hibernate, do you know he'd be able to prolong his life by surviving freezing temperatures?

Birds, alas, cannot hibernate either. They can, however, endure very cold temperatures. Even a little canary such as you might keep in a cage could survive outdoor temperatures of minus thirty degrees, or even minus fifty degrees, providing it could obtain enough food. For birds who can obtain food and who don't migrate to warmer climates, hibernation is not necessary.

The process of hibernation is controlled by a temperature-regulating center in the brain. When it becomes cold, warm-blooded animals react by sending blood from the skin to the interior of the body, by erecting their fur or feathers to improve the insulation against cold, and then by shivering, which increases the heat production.

Hibernating animals simply "turn down" this heat regulator in their bodies when it comes time to hibernate. They become practically cold-blooded animals. The process is triggered by cold temperature, a lack of food, shorter days, and other conditions.

As an animal enters hibernation, its temperature regulator becomes poor; when the body temperature falls, it doesn't respond as it normally would to keep the animal warm. Instead, the body temperature drops to conform with that of the air. Breathing becomes slow and irregular, the heart beats irregularly and slowly, and various nervous reflexes stop functioning.

If the air temperature drops to freezing, however, many hibernators begin to breathe faster and raise their heat production a bit. Some wake up. Those that don't respond at all may freeze to death.

HOW CAN PARROTS TALK?

People are amazed and delighted to hear parrots talk. But it seems that no one can yet explain how these birds are able to imitate human speech so well!

Some people think parrots can talk because of the structure of their tongue, which is large and thick. It may be that this kind of tongue does help it to talk, but it certainly isn't necessary in order for a bird to be able to talk. Other "talking" birds, such as mynas, crows, and ravens, don't have large, thick tongues. Hawks and eagles do have such tongues—and can't talk!

Is it because parrots are more intelligent than other birds? This doesn't seem to be the reason either. As a matter of fact, most biologists think that parrots and other talking birds do not realize the meaning of their own words. They do, however, seem to form definite associations between certain expressions and actions.

It may be that parrots can "talk" because their voice mechanism and hearing work more slowly than those of other birds. And probably the sounds made by human beings resemble the sounds naturally made by parrots, so it is easy for them to imitate them.

Parrots are rather remarkable birds in other ways, too. They can adapt themselves to practically any kind of living condition. This is why, for example, sailors have long taken parrots along on their trips. And even though a parrot is a tropical bird, when it is in captivity it can get along quite comfortably in temperate and even in cold climates.

Parrots are very brave birds and loyal to their kind. If a common danger threatens a group of them, the whole flock will stand by. When searching for food, they swing from one limb of a tree to another like monkeys, using their bill as well as their feet. In fact, they can use their feet at times almost like hands, especially when eating.

DO DOGS DREAM?

If you have a dog in your house, you may have noticed that when he is asleep he makes little noises and moves or twitches his legs, as though chasing something. Most dog owners who have had this experience believe this to be a sign that their dog is dreaming. While they cannot say positively that dogs do not dream, scientists will tell you that dogs probably do not dream.

To understand these scientists' theory, we must remember that men and animals are the products of evolution. This means that over millions of years gradual changes have been taking place. While men and animals are alike in some ways, the mental make-up and senses of animals have evolved in ways different from ours. As a result, animals live in worlds that are different from ours.

If the senses and the working of the minds of animals are different, we cannot expect their organs and brains to produce what our organs and brains produce. The intelligence and personality of animals are not a "miniature" of the human model.

We cannot know what thoughts animals have. So when we see what we think is a dog dreaming—moving its legs or making noises in its sleep—we cannot assume we are right. The brain cells might just be repeating their messages to the muscles, and the dog might not have any vision of a dream at all.

Those animals that have brains built something like our own may have thoughts like ours, but they will be far simpler.

WHERE DID THE RAT ORIGINATE?

Nobody likes to talk about rats, since they are unpleasant creatures. But they have had a very important effect on the life of man. In fact, the brown rat carries fleas that can spread a very dread disease: bubonic plague, or the Black Death. More people have died from this disease than from all the wars of history!

The brown rat, which is the common house rat, was originally a native of Asia. It came into Europe at about the time of the Crusades. It came partly by land, and partly on the ships that brought the Crusaders back. In a short time the brown rat was everywhere in Europe.

It came to the United States during the American Revolution, and soon spread out everywhere as the pioneers moved westward.

Why has man had such a difficult time fighting against this creature? The reason is that the rat has amazing powers of adaptation. The more prosperous man gets, the better this rat lives. Because the more food there is around, the more food it gets. When times are bad for man—and we are speaking in terms of history over the centuries—rats have a way of taking care of themselves: they become cannibals and begin to eat one another.

The brown rat is also unusually cunning. It is not fooled by the same trick twice. If poison is mixed with a food, it may kill a few rats the first time, but then the other rats learn to avoid it.

Common house rats weigh about three-quarters of a pound. They vary in color from pure gray to reddish or black-brown. Their total length is sixteen to nineteen inches. When there are other types of rats around, the brown rats drive them away and take over. They are found wherever man lives, except in the Far North and in very dry lands. Most cats, by the way, are not too good as rat-catchers.

WHAT IS A HAMSTER?

Many young people enjoy having hamsters and guinea pigs as pets. They are gentle and inquisitive rodents, easy to raise.

The golden hamster is five to six inches long and weighs four to five ounces. Its home is Europe and Asia. The name comes from the German word *hamstern,* which means "to hoard."

This is because when the hamster is wild it does just that. It stuffs its large cheek pouches with food, which it then hoards in burrows, or underground holes.

The cheek pouches can carry up to half the animal's weight in food. To empty its cheeks, the hamster presses on them with its forefeet and blows. It has a plump body and short limbs. The thick, soft fur is reddish-gold on its back and grayish-white on its belly.

The hamster is one of the fastest-reproducing mammals. It has four or five litters a year. Sometimes there are more than a dozen babies in each litter. The mother nurses the young for about four weeks.

An interesting thing about keeping hamsters as pets is that it is necessary to make it possible for them to exercise, or they will get a form of paralysis. So a hamster cage should be equipped with an exercise wheel. If the cage does not have a wheel, the hamster should be allowed out of the cage often to run and get its exercise.

WHAT IS A PARAMECIUM?

If you examine a drop of pond water under a microscope, one of the smallest creatures you may see will be longish and shaped like a slipper, rounded at one end and thin at the other. It may be hard to believe, but this tiny living thing can be classified as an animal. This is because, like all other animals, it gets food by eating plants and other organisms (plants make their own food), and it must move about to get food (plants stay in one place).

This creature is a paramecium. Its body is almost completely covered with thin, hairlike threads, which are called cilia. The cilia beat rhythmically, like thousands of tiny oars, driving the body forward or backward or in turns.

The paramecium lives in fresh water, feeding on bacteria, yeasts, and other protozoans (tiny animal-like microbes). And it seems able to control the beating of its cilia, for it can change direction rapidly to get food or avoid danger.

Like all living organisms, the paramecium can reproduce, or multiply. When it is fully grown, it may divide in two and form two new individuals. A paramecium can also reproduce by exchanging body materials with another paramecium.

The remarkable thing about the paramecium is that while it carries out many of the same living activities that humans and large animals do, it does so in a single cell. In the human body, for example, there are billions of cells, and they are organized into groups to do specific tasks.

There is a kind of specialization even in the one-celled paramecium. Inside the cell, there are two ball-shaped masses, one larger than the other. These are the nuclei. The small nucleus controls reproduction. The large one controls the other activities of the cell.

Paramecia are one of the more than one hundred thousand different kinds of micro-organisms that man has discovered and studied. (Micro-organisms are too small to be studied without a magnifying glass or microscope.) The first animals on earth may have been something like these tiny animal-like microbes.

WHAT ARE NITROGEN-FIXING BACTERIA?

Can you imagine something that is absolutely necessary to life, that is all about you, and yet that has to be "captured" to be used? This is nitrogen.

About four-fifths of the air we breathe consists of nitrogen, which is a gas. But we breathe it right out again unchanged! We only use the nitrogen to dilute the oxygen of the air so that we won't get too much at one time. Protoplasm, the substance inside all living cells, requires oxygen to be formed, and proteins, the essential food materials, are built around nitrogen compounds.

So it's pretty important for us to be able to capture nitrogen from the air. The process of doing this is called nitrogen-fixation. And a good deal of this is done for us by bacteria.

There are two kinds of nitrogen-fixing bacteria. One kind lives on the roots of plants, and the other lives free in the soil. How do they "fix" nitrogen? These bacteria take nitrogen directly from the air, combine it with oxygen, and then use this combination to build proteins.

Those that live on roots live only on the roots of plants such as beans, clover, alfalfa, and peas. But they fix more nitrogen than these plants need. The plants store the surplus in their roots. When these plants die or are harvested, the surplus nitrogen passes into the soil.

When a soil area has been used continuously for long periods of time and the plants all harvested, nitrogen is not being returned to the soil. The soil is then not able to nourish new crops. This is why farmers must use fertilizers.

The fertilizers that replace nitrogen in the soil include sodium nitrate, ammonium sulphate, and the waste products of animals and birds, such as manure. Today there are also artificial methods of nitrogen-fixation to replenish the soil.

CHAPTER 5
HOW THINGS ARE MADE

HOW IS THE CORRECT TIME DECIDED?

The two main units of time that we have are the day and the year. They are both determined by the movement of the earth. The spinning of the earth on its axis gives us the solar (sun) day. The journey of the earth around the sun gives us the solar year.

The solar day is divided into twenty-four hours. The hour is divided into sixty minutes, and the minute into sixty seconds. Actually, the length of a solar day varies. One reason for this is changes in the earth's speed around the sun. But even though each solar day is sometimes longer or sometimes shorter than exactly twenty-four hours, we say that the mean (average) solar day is twenty-four hours.

For convenience in locating places, man has marked off the earth into meridians—circles that run through the poles. Places that are on the same meridian have the same solar time. Places that are east or west of each other have different solar times. The difference in solar time is one hour for each meridian.

There is a meridian that runs through Greenwich, England, that is numbered 0. It is called the prime meridian. This is the starting point, and all other meridians are marked off east and west of Greenwich.

Clock time the whole world over is based on mean solar time at Greenwich. Astronomers at Greenwich Observatory check their clocks against the sun or a particular star. They check the exact time when the sun or the star crosses the meridian.

Observatories in other countries also keep track of the correct time. They broadcast time signals by radio. In the United States, the Naval Observatory in Washington, D.C., determines the correct time. Special clocks are used to keep the correct time. The United States Naval Observatory uses quartz-crystal controlled clocks. The electric motors in such clocks are controlled by the vibrations of the quartz crystals. The clocks keep time to within 1/500 second per day!

WHAT DO A.M. AND P.M. MEAN?

Everybody uses the expressions A.M. and P.M. to indicate before noon and after noon. But do you know exactly what they mean, and how these terms came into being?

As you know, the turning of the earth makes the sun and the stars seem to move across the sky. Daylight, of course, begins when the sun rises in the east and ends when it sets in the west. When the sun is high in the sky, between these two positions, half of the daylight hours have been spent.

Therefore, by noticing where the sun stood in the sky, early man knew he could tell the time of day. At night, the motion of the stars served the same purpose.

The important thing in keeping time is to know the exact moment of noon. For each of us, wherever we are, noon is when the sun is directly overhead. Think of an imaginary line, a meridian, drawn across the sky, stretching from the north point of your horizon down to the south point.

When the sun crosses your meridian, it is noon for you. While the sun is still east of this line or meridian, it is morning. After the sun has crossed this meridian, it is afternoon.

The Latin word for "midday" is *meridies,* from which comes our word meridian. So A.M. is an abbreviation for *ante meridiem,* or before midday. And P.M. is the abbreviation for *post meridiem,* or after midday.

Each of the world's time zones is about fifteen degrees wide in longitude, which is about the distance the sun moves through the sky in an hour. Everyone who lives in the same time zone observes noon at the same moment. In this way, the time differs by one hour as you move through each time zone.

WHY DO WATCHES HAVE JEWELS?

When a watch is advertised, the number of jewels it has is often mentioned as an indication of its quality. What exactly is a "jewel" in a watch, and why is it there?

A watch (or clock) is only useful to us if it is accurate, and if it doesn't constantly break down. The average watch contains about 211 different pieces, so obviously it's quite a complicated mechanism. Let's see what makes a watch go and the part that jewels play in this.

A watch gets its power from the mainspring, which is a coiled wire about two feet long when straightened out. When you wind the watch, you tighten the coil of the mainspring.

From the mainspring, the power travels through a series of four wheels, called the train, to the balance wheel. The train moves the hands on the dial. The balance wheel acts like the pendulum on a clock. It is the heart of the watch and regulates its movement.

Inside the balance wheel is the hairspring, a coiled steel wire no thicker than a hair. One pound of the right steel will produce eight miles of this wire!

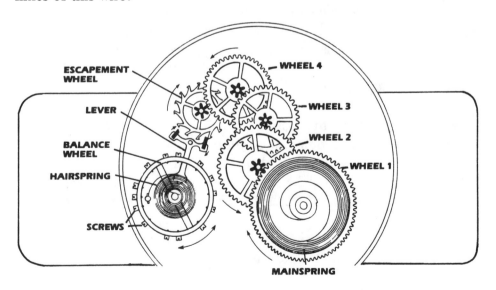

174

Around the edge of the balance wheel are adjusted tiny screws of steel or gold. Their position and weight control the speed of the watch. They are so small that an ordinary thimble will hold twenty thousand of them! Then there is the escapement wheel, which catches the balance wheel and lets it go. This regulates the movement and this is the sound that we call the "ticking" of a watch.

We've mentioned various wheels that constantly move in a watch. These wheels rest on pivots, and the constant motion creates friction. To withstand this friction, the pivots rest on tiny pieces of precious stones, such as ruby, sapphire, or garnet. These are the jewels of a watch. The more jewels, the less likely is friction to wear out or slow up the moving parts in your watch!

WHAT ARE THE PRIMARY COLORS?

If you hold up a glass prism to a beam of sunlight, you'll see the light form a rainbow of colors. This is called the spectrum. It consists of all the colors that make up "white" light.

Now, although you might be able to see six or seven colors in the spectrum, the white light is really made up of three basic colors. These are called the primary colors, because they cannot be made from any other colors. The primary colors of light are orange-red, green, and violet-blue. The other colors you see in the rainbow or spectrum are made by a mixture of the primary colors.

When the naked eye looks at the spectrum, it can see three mixed colors, which are called secondary colors. The secondary colors in light are green-blue, yellow, and magenta-red. You can produce these colors by mixing the primary colors in certain combinations.

But remember, we are talking about light. Paint colors are substances, and are exactly the opposite from light colors! The secondary colors in light are the primary colors in paint. This means that in paint the primary colors are yellow, green-blue, and magenta-red. And with these three colors, you can mix any colors in paint.

There are many other ways we classify colors. A color that is brilliant and has no black or white paint in it is called a hue. Yellow, red, blue, and green are hues. A color that is mixed from a hue and black is called a shade. Deep brown is a shade. A color that is made with a hue and white is a tint. Pink and ivory are tints. A color that is a mixture of pure hue, black, and white is a tone. Tan, beige, and gray are tones.

Here is an interesting fact about color. How do you think red paint looks before the can is opened? It doesn't look red. It actually looks black! That's because where there is no light, there is no color. In a dark room, there is no such thing as color.

The color of an object depends on the material of the object and the light in which the object is seen. For instance, an orange-red sweater looks orange-red because the dye in the wool reflects the orange-red part of the light. The violet-blue and green parts of light are absorbed by the sweater. Only the orange-red is reflected for you to see.

WHAT MAKES HOT AND COLD?

Some things are hot to the touch, other things are cold. Sometimes the air feels hot, other times it feels cool. What makes the difference?

According to present theories, heat consists of the motion of atoms and molecules. For example, the atoms and molecules in the air are able to move about freely, bumping into each other and into objects in their path. Now, these tiny particles may move rapidly or slowly. If they move rapidly, we say the temperature of the air is high, or that the air is hot. If they move slowly (as on a cold day), we feel the air to be cool.

When it comes to liquids and solids, the atoms and molecules cannot move so freely—but they are still able to move rapidly. For example, in a block of hot iron the atoms vibrate perhaps a million times each second—and that's rapidly! If you were to touch the tip of your finger to such a block, you would feel pain because of the sudden and violent motion imparted to the molecules in your skin when they come near the fast-moving particles of the iron.

Do molecules really move about? Countless experiments prove that the molecules actually do move constantly. In fact, under the microscope tiny particles of matter in water can be seen being knocked around by millions of invisible molecules in motion.

At the temperature of melting ice, on the average, an oxygen molecule moves with a speed of about one thousand four hundred feet per second; and a hydrogen molecule about four times as fast. Even in a cubic inch of air a thousand million million collisions per second take place among the molecules!

Heat and temperature are not the same thing. The heat energy a body contains depends upon the energy of motion of its atoms and molecules. The quantity of heat may be measured in "calories." A calorie is the amount of heat energy required to raise the temperature of one gram of water one degree centigrade. But the temperature of a body indicates the level or "degree" to which the heat energy that it contains brings it. The coldest temperature possible is 273 degrees below zero centigrade. Scientists believe that at that temperature the molecules are at rest.

HOW DO FIREWORKS GET THEIR COLORS?

Fireworks have been making people say "Ahh!" and "Ohh!" for thousands of years. The magnificent displays of the Chinese delighted their people hundreds of years before fireworks appeared in western Europe.

The Greeks had some sort of fireworks known as "Greek fire," and Roman emperors put on elaborate exhibitions of fireworks to amuse the people. But fireworks didn't really develop as we know them until gunpowder came into general use and the science of chemistry had made certain advances.

In the nineteenth century the art of making fireworks was really perfected, and amazingly elaborate displays were created. For instance, certain fireworks were shot into the sky in which beautiful colored designs served as a backdrop. Other pieces were attached to frameworks against this background. When these fireworks were lit, unbelievable patterns were produced, such as waving flags, rushing trains and steamboats, and even mock battles between famous people!

The basic materials used in making fireworks are saltpeter, sulfur and charcoal. These ingredients are ground together into a fine powder and then nitrates of lead, barium, and aluminum are sometimes added in various combinations to obtain spectacular effects.

The colors in fireworks are produced by the addition of various salts of metals. Strontium produces red, barium creates green, sodium is for yellow, and copper for blue. The showers of dazzling sparks are made by using iron filings. So you see it takes quite a knowledge of chemistry to produce our modern fireworks.

Of course, there is a serious side to fireworks, too. In warfare, rockets are used for signaling, and flares can light up whole battlefields or convey messages. At sea, various colored flares and rockets have often been the means for saving hundreds of lives. And pilots in airplanes have often been able to make emergency landings, thanks to flares dropped from the plane.

CAN A THERMOMETER BE MADE WITHOUT MERCURY?

We are so accustomed to thinking of a thermometer as having mercury in a thin tube that we tend to forget exactly how a thermometer works.

A thermometer is simply an instrument that measures heat. The way we measure heat is by observing what heat does to certain materials. Heat causes many materials to change. We look at what kind of change has taken place in the material, and we can say that this kind of change was caused by a certain amount of heat.

The reason mercury is used so commonly in thermometers is simply because mercury reacts quickly to a rise in temperature. It expands evenly, and it is easily seen. So in the modern mercury-in-glass thermometer, heat causes the mercury to expand; it moves up the narrow tube, and a scale on the thermometer tells us how high it has moved.

Alcohol, for example, can also be used in thermometers. But alcohol presents certain problems. It boils easily. So alcohol is not very useful for high temperatures. But alcohol makes an excellent thermometer for measuring extremely low temperatures.

There are other kinds of thermometers that use no liquid at all. Instead, two metals are used. A strip of iron and a strip of brass are fastened together in the form of a coil. One end of this coil is fastened, while the other end is connected to a pointer and is free to move.

The metals expand and contract at different rates. When heated, the free end of the coil winds or unwinds, as the case may be, and this movement positions a pointer on a dial with degrees on it.

By placing a pen on the pointer and by providing a rotating chart, we have a recording thermometer that keeps a record of the temperature for as long as we want it to!

WHAT IS THE LAW OF FALLING BODIES?

A falling body is an unsupported object that is being pulled toward the earth's surface by the force of gravity. Gravity is the earth's force of attraction for other objects.

When there is no air resistance, all bodies fall according to a definite law. It is known as the law of falling bodies, and was first discovered by the famous Italian scientist Galileo in the 1500's.

Galileo experimented with falling bodies in his laboratory. Out of these experiments came this new law: In the absence of air, the speed of a falling body depends only on the length of the fall. The speed of the body does not depend on the body's weight.

The longer a body falls, the faster and faster it moves. When anything picks up speed, we say it accelerates. A freely-falling body has an acceleration of thirty-two feet a second during each second that it falls. This means that for each second a body falls, it gains thirty-two feet a second in downward speed.

A falling body has a speed of thirty-two feet a second after falling for just one second. It has a speed of thirty-two plus thirty-two, or sixty-four feet a second after falling for two seconds, and so on.

However, a body falling through the air does not continue to gain speed at this rate. It reaches a certain top speed. Because of air resistance, there is a limit to how fast an object falls.

This is true of even the heaviest objects. They accelerate as they begin to fall, but air resistance builds up. Soon the air resistance becomes equal to the pull of gravity on the object. Then the object can fall no faster. It has reached its final or "terminal speed," and keeps this speed as it continues to fall.

WHAT MAKES A BALLOON RISE?

A balloon is really the simplest form of aircraft. It usually consists of a light spherical or cylindrical bag made of paper, rubber, silk, or rubberized fabric, containing hot air, hydrogen, or helium. To the bag may be attached (by cords or netting) a basket, or car, or gondola to carry passengers and cargo.

A balloon floats in the air for exactly the same reason that a fish floats in water. Each displaces, by its bulk, more than its own weight of the air or water that surrounds it.

As long as a balloon and all the equipment attached to it weigh less than the volume of air displaced, it will rise. If it loses some of its lifting gas, so that its volume decreases, it will sink. Hot air, hydrogen, or helium are used as lifting gases because all three are lighter than ordinary atmospheric air.

Once released, a balloon will ascend to a level where the weight of the displaced air is exactly equal to its own weight. To change flight altitude, a balloon pilot must either reduce his buoyancy to go down, or reduce his weight to go up. To go down, he must allow some of his lifting gas to escape through a valve in the top of the balloon. To go up, he must throw weights (ballasts) overboard.

Since neither gas nor ballasts can be replaced in flight, it is easy to see that the amount of control available to a balloon pilot is quite limited. At best, he can go up or down for a short time only, depending on the size of the balloon.

Once aloft, he is entirely at the mercy of the winds. A balloon cannot be steered in flight. It can only drift with the wind, and for this reason has very little use as a means of getting from place to place.

Balloons are now generally used for upper-air exploration. In warfare they are commonly used as elevated observation posts. They may form balloon barrages (like aerial fences) to protect cities from bombers.

WHAT MAKES AN AIRPLANE STALL IN THE AIR?

To understand this, we must first understand what enables an airplane to stay up in the air. Because an airplane weighs more than the same volume of air, it needs some force to hold it up. This force is called lift.

An airplane develops lift by moving forward against the air swiftly. How does this motion create lift? It has to do with the flow of air past the wings. The air flows over and under the wings as the plane moves forward. The air under the wings pushes up against the wings. The air over the wings is forced into a slight upward curve over the wings, which creates an area of decreased pressure. So we have two effects working together: the air under the wings pushes up; the decreased pressure above the wings helps draw the wings up. The result is lift.

In order for the plane to move forward, it uses engine power. The propellers screw forward into the air just as a wood screw does in wood. This is possible because when air moves swiftly, or something moves swiftly into it, the air begins to act like a solid. This forward pull of the plane is called thrust. The thrust overcomes the "drag" exerted by the plane, the lift overcomes gravity, and the plane is able to stay in the air.

As long as the upward lift and the pull of gravity downward are exactly equal, the plane flies level and straight. If the speed is increased, the plane will climb because there is more lift, so the pilot must turn the plane's nose down.

When the speed is reduced, the pilot must bring the nose up. If the speed is reduced and the nose is not brought up, the air becomes "burbly," and the lift is lost. The nose drops, the plane stalls, and may go into a spin.

When a stall takes place high above the ground, there is enough altitude to enable the plane to recover and regain speed, but a stall near the ground may result in a crash.

WHAT IS A SEXTANT?

When you travel by land, you can usually find your way because you know where a road leads. And if you travel by ship and can see the shore, you can also find your location easily. You can recognize hills, mountains, forests, beaches, and so on.

In the earliest times, therefore, sailors kept their ships within two or three miles of the coast, so that they were never out of sight of land. The men who did venture out into the ocean were taking a great risk because there was no sure way of knowing their location.

Later, a way was found to pinpoint the location of ships at sea. This was done by finding the latitude and longitude of the place. Latitude is distance north or south of the Equator. Longitude tells how far east or west a place is, and it is measured by degrees east or west of an imaginary line that goes through Greenwich, England.

To find latitude and longitude at sea, the navigator observes the position of the stars and the sun. In the daytime, the navigator can find the latitude of his ship by measuring how high the sun is at noon. At night, he does this by measuring how high in the sky the stars seem to be. Longitude is measured by comparing the time on board the ship with the time at Greenwich, England. If his time is earlier, he is west of Greenwich; if later, he is east of Greenwich. Each hour's difference equals fifteen degrees east or west.

The sextant is an instrument used by navigators to measure the position of the sun, moon, planets, and certain stars. The sextant is shaped like the wedge of a pie, with a scale marked on its rounded edge.

One end of a swinging arm is attached to the point of the sextant. A movable mirror is fixed at that end of the arm. The other end extends to the scale. A telescope is mounted on the sextant, and a glass mirror is mounted in front of the telescope. By looking at the horizon through the telescope and a clear glass, and then moving the mirror until the reflection seems to touch the horizon, the scale end shows the height of the body observed.

HOW DO WE KNOW THE HEIGHT
OF A MOUNTAIN?

When we read of high mountains in newspapers or books, we are often told their exact height in terms of feet. How do we know exactly how high a mountain is, especially in the case of mountains that may never have been climbed by man?

It is done by means of one of the oldest techniques on earth—surveying. The science of surveying is a branch of civil engineering. It is concerned with determining the shape and size of any part of the earth's surface.

There are various kinds of surveying, but they are all based on a method known as "triangulation." When you study geometry, you will learn that if you know one side and two angles of any triangle (or two sides and one angle), you can find out the rest of its measurements.

Whether the land you want to measure is one acre, or a thousand acres, the method of measuring it is the same. You begin by measuring one distance very accurately with a chain, steel rod, or wire.

This now becomes the side of the first triangle, and is usually a level piece of ground between two landmarks. Now you select a third landmark, and make this the apex of the triangle. You then measure the angles it makes with each end of the first line you measured. You now have the requirements for measuring the area of the triangle as described above (one side and two angles of a triangle).

The instrument for measuring those angles is called a transit. Now that you have the area of one triangle, you keep on dividing the land to be measured into triangles until you have the area of the entire piece of land.

The transit doesn't just work horizontally; it also works vertically. This is called leveling, because there is a spirit level at the base of the instrument that indicates when it is level. By raising the sight to any landmark on a mountain, the same process of measuring angles can be done, and the length of one side (the height) can be measured!

HOW DOES AN AQUALUNG WORK?

The aqualung is a modern aid to diving. It makes it possible for a diver to go on breathing underwater without an air supply from a ship. He carries his own air supply with him, strapped to his back. He is a free diver.

For air supply the aqualung has two or more sturdy steel bottles filled with compressed air. A special valve gradually lets the air out of the bottles. A hose from the valve goes to a mouthpiece. This is made so that the diver can grip it with his teeth. Because the diver's nose is covered with his faceplate, he has to breathe through his mouth.

With the aqualung strapped to his back and a heavy belt to keep him down, a man can swim almost as freely as a fish. He uses big flippers on his feet, so he doesn't need his hands for swimming. He can hold a camera or perhaps a fishing spear. In shallow water he may be able to stay down for a half-hour or more.

But even the best free-diving outfit will not let a diver go down more than three hundred feet. At this depth the weight of the water above presses on everything ten times as heavily as on the surface. The air in the diver's bottles is used up ten times as fast. So even big bottles will let him stay there for only one minute or so.

There is another problem in deep diving. The compressed air in the aqualung bottles is about four-fifths nitrogen and about one-fifth oxygen, like ordinary air. We need the oxygen to stay alive. Ordinarily the nitrogen we breathe in is breathed right out again. But as the pressure of air increases, some of the nitrogen dissolves in the blood and tissues.

As the diver comes up, the nitrogen must leave his blood and tissues. If it cannot come out fast enough through his lungs, it turns into tiny bubbles inside his body. The bubbles squeeze nerves and block blood vessels, and the diver gets what is called the bends. The diver feels great pain. A bad case of the bends may kill him or cripple him for life.

This is why a diver must come up quite slowly when he is down to a depth of two hundred or three hundred feet. And he must stop often on the way up.

HOW IS WATER MADE DRINKABLE?

First of all, why does water have to be made drinkable? Why can't we drink it just as we find it? The reason is that we can almost never obtain pure water.

Probably the purest natural source of water is snow. The next purest is rain water, but rain contains dissolved gases of the air and traces of carbon dioxide, chlorides, sulfates, nitrates, and ammonia. Even the water from streams and lakes that are found in the mountains may contain dissolved inorganic salts. Water from rivers and lakes in low regions is usually quite polluted. Water from springs and wells has filtered through the ground, so it is quite pure, but it may also contain inorganic salts.

So it seems that all water we drink needs to be purified to some degree. There are many methods for doing this. One is simply by storage. When water is stored in a reservoir, certain things take place. Solid impurities settle at the bottom, a process known as sedimentation. Many bacteria lose their power when water is kept in a storage reservoir.

But this method does not give complete protection. So chemicals may be added to provide better sedimentation. In addition, the water may be aerated to remove tastes and odors and dissolved gases.

Many years ago it was discovered that if water could be filtered through sand, many of the impurities and most of the bacteria could be removed. So various methods for sand-filtering were set up, including a method that forced the water through mechanically at great speed.

A commonly used method for purifying water is chlorination. This is a very cheap, quick, and effective method. From two to eight pounds of chlorine are added to a million gallons of water. This is enough to destroy most of the dangerous bacteria that may be in the water.

HOW IS FASHION DECIDED?

The French word *couturier* means "dressmaker." In the world of fashion, the word has come to describe a designer of high fashion or *haute couture*. It is these designers who begin trends and create new silhouettes. The work of famous couturiers of different countries is copied all over the world.

Paris has always been the traditional center of world fashion. But recently Italian designers have had great influence in setting new styles, and so have certain designers in London.

French designers guard the secrets of their new designs until their collections are shown to the public. Then pictures of the styles are published in newspapers and magazines all over the world.

People from many countries travel to Paris to buy the clothes and to copy the newest ideas. In January they come to see the spring clothes; in July, to see the fall designs.

Many dress manufacturers from other countries buy the original clothes of the famous French designers. They take them back to their own design rooms, where the clothes are copied line-for-line to be made in great numbers. That's why you may be able to buy in your town the clothing that is in the latest style without paying a very high price for it.

Some manufacturers use the Paris styles only as a starting point for their own ideas. Others may adapt only a part of the French design into their own styles.

The United States has become one of the most important fashion centers in the world. In New York City, there are American designers who create new fashions and show their collections. Buyers from stores all over the world come to New York to buy the clothes.

After the buyers choose the designs, the dress manufacturers add up the store orders, buy fabrics, and have the dresses sewn by machines. They are then shipped to cities all over the United States and the world.

WHAT IS LIPSTICK?

Like so many other cosmetics in use today, lipstick is a product of the chemist's laboratory. Every ingredient that goes into it has a definite purpose, and the combination makes quite a complicated formula.

The chief ingredients in a lipstick are castor oil and a mixture of various waxes. In addition there are cacao butter, lanolin, mineral oil, petrolatum, and different chemicals. Coloring matter to obtain the exact shade is, of course, a very important ingredient.

The oils and waxes are melted together and the colors mixed in by grinding. The whole mass is then remelted and poured into molds, where it is allowed to harden. Lipsticks are made so that they will soften under pressure, which makes it possible to apply them to the lips evenly.

The use of cosmetics by women goes back to very early times. They probably originated in the East, but in ancient times they reached their greatest development in Egypt. Almost six thousand years ago various kinds of cosmetics were already being used in Egypt.

Cleopatra carried the use of cosmetics to new heights. At that time, it was the eyes that received the most attention. Women of the court painted the under side of the eye green, and the lid, lashes, and eyebrows black! Henna was also used to dye the fingernails, palms, and soles of the feet.

In the Bible there are many references to the use of cosmetics by women—for example, "When Jehu was come to Jezreel, Jezebel heard of it; and she painted her face. . . ."

In Rome, at the time of Nero, cosmetics and perfumes were widely used. Here are some of the cosmetics they had then: white lead and chalk to whiten the skin; paint for the eyelids and lashes; a rouge for the cheeks and lips, which may be the ancestor of our lipstick;

barley flour and butter as a cure for blemishes; and pumice stone for whitening the teeth. They also had a kind of soap for bleaching the hair.

In England, about four hundred years ago, women used to take all kinds of baths to make their skin beautiful. It is said that Mary, Queen of Scots, actually bathed in wine, and other women of the time took milk baths!

WHAT IS LACE?

Lace is an airy and delicate fabric made of fine threads stitched into patterns. Lace is used to add beauty to many of the things we wear and use. It may be made by hand or by machine.

The first true hand-made lace was probably made in Italy in the middle of the 1500's. Very soon afterward, laces were being made in France. Today hand-made lace is made chiefly in Italy and Belgium. Machine-made lace is produced in England, France, and the United States.

Hand-made lace is usually made by one of two methods: needle-point or bobbin. Needlepoint lace is made by drawing the design on a thick piece of paper backed by linen. The outline of the pattern is stitched onto the paper. The stitching is used as a framework on which the lacemaker works with a needle and single thread, building up the pattern with looped stitches. When the work is completed, the framework stitches are clipped and the lace is lifted off the pattern.

Bobbin lace is made with a large number of threads, each fastened to a bobbin (spool). The pattern is drawn on paper, and the paper is fastened onto a cushion. Then pins are stuck into the cushion to keep the threads in position while the lace is being made. The lace is made with a pair of bobbins in each hand. These are moved from side to side to twist or interlace the threads. As the work progresses, the pins are moved farther along.

Chantilly lace is a bobbin lace that has vine or spray patterns on a mesh ground; it is often used on evening dresses and bridal veils. Cluny lace is a fairly coarse bobbin lace; it is often used to trim children's dresses and household linens.

WHAT IS EMBROIDERY?

Embroidery is the art of sewing decorative stitches on cloth. It is a very old art. Evidences of embroidered clothing have been found by archaeologists digging among ancient Assyrian and Persian ruins. The Old Testament describes the beauty of the embroidery done by the Jews in Biblical times.

In the Middle Ages embroidery reached a high point. Great Italian and Dutch painters designed needlework tapestries illustrating religious subjects. Noblewomen spent many hours in their castles embroidering gowns to be worn on state occasions, or altar cloths and hangings for the church.

One of the most famous medieval embroideries is the Bayeux tapestry, which illustrates the Battle of Hastings. Its warriors and horses, griffins, phoenixes, and monsters are worked in eight shades of wool on a linen strip measuring 230 feet long and nearly 20 inches wide.

During the eighteenth century embroideries became so valuable that they were worth more than their weight in gold! In the 1700's and 1800's, little girls in America had to spend a certain amount of time each day learning to embroider. They practiced different stitches on a piece of linen that was called a sampler. Houses, animals, numbers, the letters of the alphabet, and sometimes verses were embroidered on the sampler. When the stitching was finished, the little girl added her name, her age, and the date.

Each country has its own style of embroidery. The Chinese and Japanese use silk and gold threads on fine damask to embroider dragons, birds, flowers, and landscapes. Warm countries, such as Spain and Italy, produce embroideries that are gay in color and pattern.

France and Switzerland are noted for the most delicate kind of needlework, often embroidered in plain white. In the Balkan countries embroidery of fine stitches in vivid colors decorates clothing and linens that are passed on from generation to generation.

WHAT IS KAPOK?

Today, chemists are able to create all kinds of wonderful products in their laboratories. So many of them appear on the market under various names that we sometimes forget that Nature herself is able to turn out some pretty interesting products, too! Kapok is one of these.

Kapok is the product of a tree of the bombax family that is cultivated in Java, the Philippines, Malay, and Ceylon. The tree is native to the West Indies and other parts of tropical America.

Since this tree can be grown under widely different conditions, many varieties of it have been developed. In fact, there are now at least fifty-four different trees that produce what we call kapok, and some of these trees yield crops for fifty years or longer.

What is kapok? It looks like fine, yellowish, shiny cotton. It grows in fat pods on these tall trees. The growing kapok fibers are not attached to the seeds, so ginning (as with cotton) is not necessary.

The cleaned kapok fiber, which is called floss, is springy, slick, and odorless. It sheds water like a duck's back, and resists the passage of sound and heat. It is half as heavy as wool and just as warm. High-quality floss supports as much as thirty-eight times its own weight in water.

Each kapok fiber is a smooth closed tube coated with wax. Not having the twist that grows in cotton fibers or the hooks found in sheep's wool, kapok won't mat or felt, and cannot be spun into threads.

Kapok-stuffed life preservers support six times as much weight as those filled with cork. They last three to five times as long without getting waterlogged. In wartime, kapok is used to line tanks, trench coats, and sleeping bags. In peacetime, it is used to insulate refrigerators and airplanes, and in softballs, boxing gloves, mattresses, and upholstery. The seeds of the kapok tree yield an oil that is used in food and in making soap.

WHAT IS ORIGAMI?

You have probably enjoyed many, many times just sitting around and folding pieces of paper to make them look like a bird, a ship, or some animal. What you probably didn't realize is that you were practicing a very ancient "art," the art of paper folding, or origami.

The Chinese invented paper almost two thousand years ago, and origami is just as old as paper itself. It is possible that the art developed from an ancient custom: the Chinese funeral rite of making paper houses, furniture, vehicles, and servants, as well as paper money. In fact, at Buddhist funerals colored-paper symbols of all kinds of things are burned. The idea is that the dead person will enjoy all the comforts that are symbolized by the paper objects in the next world.

In the seventh century paper folding was brought to Japan. The Japanese developed many of China's arts and crafts into their own forms of expression. They found new methods of folding paper into pretty forms and images, and made origami a highly creative art.

From a few simple folds the Japanese make things of great beauty and realism. Some decorate the shrines and temples as religious symbols. Others, such as the crane, tortoise, and lobster, are good-luck symbols. These are fastened to gifts as ornaments or used as festive decorations.

Japanese magicians, traveling in Europe, introduced paper folding to the western world. The magicians were so expert that with a few quick movements they could make a bird, animal, or insect to surprise and delight the audience.

Did you know that many great men of the past not only enjoyed origami, but also became very good at it? Among these people were Leonardo da Vinci, the poet Shelley, and the writer Lewis Carroll, the author of *Alice in Wonderland*.

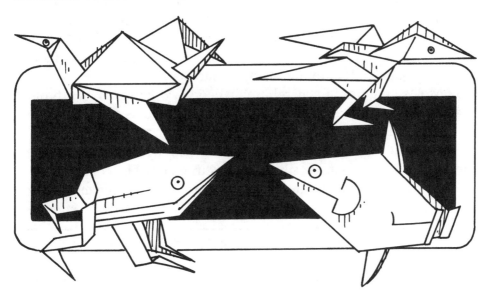

WHAT ARE DIES AND MOLDS?

Many of the things we see and use every day are made with dies or molds.

Dies are special tools that shape and cut metal and plastic by pressure. If you have ever watched as star-shaped cookies were punched out of a sheet of dough by a cookie cutter, you have seen a very simple type of die in action.

Molds are special tools used to shape materials in liquid form. Metal, plastic, or whatever other material is used is poured or forced into the cavity of the mold and is allowed to solidify. A mold of gelatin is an example of a very simple type of mold.

Dies are used in industry to make parts with shapes that are hard to produce with other machine tools. Examples are automobile parts, such as hoods and fenders.

Molds are also used in industry to make parts, such as refrigerator-door handles, radio casings, and some automobile radiator grilles.

To make parts like these by regular machine operations of cutting, grinding, and drilling would take a great deal of time and much material would be wasted. With dies they can be stamped out like cookies. The same holds true for molds.

In addition to producing difficult shapes, dies and molds are good for fast production of large numbers of identical parts. The parts that dies and molds turn out usually need no finishing. Difficult parts may require a little grinding or polishing to remove seams on molded parts and rough edges on die-stamped parts.

Molds and dies in general are made in two halves. When brought together they will make the shape of the part. Molds form the outside shape only. Dies can form both the inside and outside shapes.

Did you know that dies were used as long ago as 650 B.C., when Greek metalworkers made silver coins with them? The coins were produced by pounding metal into a pattern cut into a harder metal block.

WHAT IS CERAMICS?

In a museum you can see vases, jars, cups, and dishes—all pieces of pottery. Pottery is clay that has been shaped when soft, then hardened by heat. The art of making such products is called ceramics.

The word "ceramics" is sometimes used for enamel and glass, as well as pottery. In all three cases the work involves applying heat to earthy materials—clay, sand, or ground rock.

Ceramics is one of the oldest of man's arts. Clay is found almost everywhere. Pieces of ceramic work have been found that date from before the beginning of recorded history. A well-hardened piece of pottery is very durable. It may break, but it will not rot or rust away.

The outstanding early potters were the Chinese. They made a very hard and translucent type of pottery known as porcelain. In the West, porcelain became known as china, after the country that first produced it.

There are six main groups of clay that are used in ceramics. The first is called common clay, and is not used for making fine pottery. The pottery made from common clay is called earthenware.

The purest type of clay is called kaolin, or china clay. It is used to make Chinese porcelain. When fired, it turns a pure white.

Many years ago, before refrigeration was developed, ceramic jugs (called "crockery") were used to keep liquids cool. This is because crockery is a coarse type of ceramics that permits liquids to seep through its tiny pores. The liquid then evaporates on the outside. And the constant evaporation of the moisture keeps the jug and its contents cool.

Today, however, most crockery is glazed and has a shiny surface; this doesn't allow this kind of evaporation to take place.

WHAT IS CONCRETE?

Concrete is one of the most useful building materials ever developed by man. It is strong, long-lasting, fairly cheap to use, and easy to handle. It is not harmed by fire, water, weather, or heavy pressures. Huge dams, bridges, and skyscrapers, as well as highways, homes, and airport runways, are built of concrete.

Concrete is made from Portland cement, water, and sand, gravel, or crushed stone. The materials are measured and mixed together to make concrete. After mixing, the concrete can be given any shape that is wanted by placing it in molds that are called forms.

The mixing turns the water and cement into a paste that coats the pieces of sand and gravel. When this paste hardens, it holds the pieces together in a solid, rock-like mass. Keeping the concrete moist after putting it in the forms makes it even harder. Because of a chemical reaction between the cement and the water, the concrete keeps getting harder as it ages.

Concrete is treated in various ways to make it suitable for special purposes. For example, when concrete is used in long, slender parts, it may snap or be pulled apart. To make concrete structures hold up under forces that would bend them or pull them apart, steel rods or mesh can be set in the concrete. This is called reinforced concrete.

Concrete can also be strengthened by casting (pouring) it around high-tension steel wires. When these wires are tightened—before the concrete hardens—they place the concrete in a squeeze that makes it stronger. Such concrete is called prestressed concrete.

A kind of concrete is now made that contains billions of tiny air bubbles in each cubic inch. It is called air-entrained concrete. Highways built of this concrete are not harmed by freezing and thawing.

So you can see how much can be done with concrete to make it serve special needs in construction.

HOW MANY KINDS OF NAILS ARE THERE?

Nails are usually used for joining pieces of wood or for fastening other materials to wood. Nails are simply hammered into place and are held there by friction. Some nails have roughened shanks so that they will hold better.

Most nails are made by machine from heavy steel wire. These machines can make hundreds of nails per minute. First the machine cuts the wire to the correct length. Then it flattens one end of the wire to make the head. And finally, it cuts the point at the other end.

Some types of nails, called cut nails, are stamped, or cut, from sheets of metal. Cut nails are rectangular, rather than round.

There is a tremendous variety of nails, since they are used for so many different purposes. The ordinary all-purpose nails most of us use are called common nails. Finishing nails, used in furniture and cabinetwork, have very small heads that do not show on the finished work.

Roofing nails have very large heads. They are used for nailing shingles or tar paper to a roof. The large head holds the thin material and keeps it from tearing loose.

Some nails have two heads, one above the other. The nail is driven only as far as the first head. The top head of the nail remains above the surface of the work, to make it easy to pull the nail out. Two-headed nails are used to hold scaffolding and other temporary structures together.

Most nails are made of steel. Masonry nails, used on concrete or masonry, are made of specially hardened steel. Some nails, such as roofing nails, are galvanized. That means they are coated with zinc to prevent rusting.

Nails used on boats must be extra rustproof. They are usually made of brass or bronze. Large nails are called spikes, and are usually over six inches long.

WHAT IS A DREDGE?

The water in harbors, rivers, and lakes often contains a large amount of mud and silt, which settle on the bottom. If enough of this material builds up, the water becomes too shallow for ships to use. To keep the waterways open, the mud and silt must be scooped up and removed from time to time. The machines used for this are called dredges.

Some of these dredges are mounted on ship hulls and can sail about under their own power. Others are mounted on floating platforms that have to be towed about in the water.

Dredges use several different kinds of power. Suction dredges, which suck up mud and silt like a vacuum cleaner, are usually driven by steam turbines or diesel engines. Some dredges use electric power supplied from the shore. Dipper dredges operate by means of steam or diesel power.

A dipper dredge is a seagoing version of the common steam shovel. A dipper on the end of a dipper stick is attached to a long boom that can be raised and lowered. The steel cutting teeth of the dipper bite into the mud. When the boom is raised and swung over a barge, the hinged bottom of the dipper opens and dumps its load into the barge.

A kind of dredge known as a grab dredge has two types of buckets: the "clamshell" and the "orange peel." The clamshell bucket has two hinged parts that open to scoop up the mud. The orange-peel bucket has three hinged parts.

The ladder-type bucket dredge scoops up mud and silt with an endless chain of buckets. The buckets are mounted on a long steel frame, which is lowered to the bottom. As each bucket reaches the bottom, it fills with mud and silt. It travels back to the surface, and at the top of the frame it up-ends, spilling its load onto a barge.

Ladder bucket dredges are also used in mining operations in swampy areas in Alaska, California, South America, and many other places. They dig up the earth and feed it into huge washing cylinders that separate out the ore.

HOW DOES AN OIL DERRICK WORK?

When you think about drilling for oil, you may imagine a tall steel structure with black oil gushing out of it. But gushers are a thing of the past. Modern drilling methods have practically eliminated them.

Many kinds of oil derricks are used. Some are as tall as a twenty-story office building, others are attached to trucks, and still others are located on platforms and barges for offshore drilling.

Rotary drilling accounts for about 85 percent of the wells in the United States. Rotary drilling uses a rapidly-turning bit that bores into the earth. Different kinds of bits are used for different kinds of rock. Attached to the bit is a drilling pipe in thirty-foot sections called joints, each weighing about five hundred pounds.

A flat steel turntable grips and turns the pipe, which extends through it into the earth. As the pipe turns, the bit attached to it cuts into the earth. Section after section of pipe is added as the drill chews its way downward.

During the drilling, "drilling mud" is pumped down inside the pipe, which cools and lubricates the bit. As the hole deepens, a long steel pipe, called casing, is added from time to time.

Cutting through rock dulls the bit, so it must be replaced often. This means all the drill pipe must be pulled out of the hole. There is a lot of work involved in this, and it may take four to six hours to replace the bit and put the pipe down again.

When a well has reached a certain depth, the bit and drill are pulled up, and casing is run all the way down and filled with chemical mud. A small gun is lowered to make holes in the casing and start the oil flowing. Later, water is pumped in to get rid of the mud. Pressure begins to rise from the well, and finally oil begins to bubble out of valves into an open tank.

HOW DOES A GEIGER COUNTER WORK?

You've probably read about a modern type of "prospector" who goes out looking for precious metals with a Geiger counter. Or perhaps, when people are talking about the danger of atom bombs, there is mention of using Geiger counters as a safety measure.

In both cases, what is involved is the matter of radiation. Certain radioactive substances give off rays, and a Geiger counter is a simple way of detecting and measuring these rays. The Geiger counter was invented by Hans Geiger, and later perfected by a man called Müller.

It is really a kind of vacuum tube. In simple terms, the tube consists of a very thin glass envelope, much like an ordinary radio tube. Inside are two metal plates and a small amount of gas, such as argon.

You're familiar with another kind of tube that contains a gas—the neon tube. In the neon tube or lamp, the gas can be made to glow by connecting the plates to a source of electrical voltage, providing this voltage is high enough. The high voltage breaks the gas down and allows a large flow of electrons to take place between the plates. And when this flow takes place, the gas inside the tube begins to glow.

In a Geiger counter, the voltage is deliberately kept too low so that the glow of the gas won't take place under normal conditions. Now, let's assume there is some radioactive substance nearby. A ray from this radioactive substance enters the tube and collides with the gas molecules. This gives them enough energy (just as higher voltage would) to cause the gas to glow.

So now there is a current surging through the tube. This current can be put through an indicating meter so that you can read the amount of radiation that has entered the tube. Or, it can be made to produce that familiar ticking sound that is associated with Geiger counters.

Since a Geiger counter is a means of detecting radiation, it obviously can't detect anything that doesn't emit rays. So its use is limited in searching for precious metals.

HOW DO ESCALATORS WORK?

An escalator is basically a set of moving stairs.

Each step is loosely connected to the next step by two very heavy roller chains. This is so that the steps can rise and sink easily. Each step has axles with wheels or rollers on them. The wheels rest on metal tracks inside a steel frame called a truss. The truss rests between two floors like a steeply slanted ladder. In fact, the word "escalator" was made up from a Latin word meaning ladder.

The steps lie flat at each end of the escalator. This is to make it easier for passengers to get on and off. As the steps travel up or down the escalator, they automatically rise so that they look like steps in a staircase. As the steps approach the end of the ride, they automatically flatten out again.

Under the floor at the top end of the escalator is a set of sprockets. A sprocket is a wheel with projecting teeth, like the gear wheel of a bicycle.

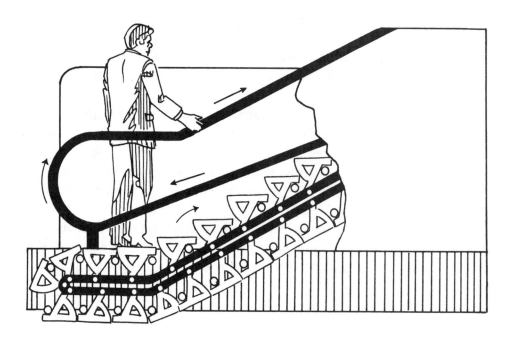

The teeth of the sprocket catch the links of the roller chain and drive it around and around, pulling the steps along their rails. The sprocket at the top end of the escalator is driven by an electric motor beneath the floor. The chains run over pulleys at the bottom. These pulleys steer the chains properly and keep them tight.

At each side of the moving steps is a protective wall called a balustrade to keep passengers from falling off the sides of the steps. On top of the balustrade is a moving endless belt of rubber or metal, which is the handrail passengers hold onto to keep their balance.

The first escalator was patented in the United States in 1859, but it wasn't used commercially. The first practical escalator was built in 1891.

HOW ARE BELLS RUNG?

For hundreds of years bells in church towers have been rung for a variety of purposes. Bells reminded Christians of the relation of the church to their daily lives. They would be rung at daybreak to wake people up and call them to morning prayers. Through the day the bells counted the hours, the half-hours, and the quarters. They pealed for weddings and tolled for funerals, and were heard at Easter and Christmas.

A bell may be rung in two ways: the bell may be swung to hit the clapper; or the bell may be struck by the clapper or by some outside object. In the Far East some big stationary bells are rung by striking them with a log in the manner of a battering ram. One such bell in Burma weighs about ninety tons.

The Russians once cast a giant bell that weighed twice as much, but it cracked. To ring such a bell requires several men pulling a rope attached to the clapper.

In England a different method of bell-ringing was developed, called change-ringing. In change-ringing, the bells swing in complete circles in a definite order. The bells sound variations, or changes, on a descending scale. There is no melody, only a rhythmic pattern, and it can go on for hours.

There are over five thousand towers in England, each containing a set of bells for change-ringing. A set can number from three to twelve bells, and each bell is swung by one ringer using a rope and wheel.

A bell known as a clock-bell originated in the monasteries of Europe. This was because the monastic day was divided into devotional periods called canonical hours. In some monasteries the bell had to be rung seven times in twenty-four hours.

Since the first clock-bells could not ring by themselves, a man was hired for the job of striking them at the proper times of day. But in time he was replaced by machinery. With machinery it was possible to ring many bells, and it became customary to ring a short tune as a warning that the hour bell was about to strike.

HOW DOES A SATELLITE TRANSMIT TV PROGRAMS?

An artificial satellite is a man-made spacecraft circling the earth. Such satellites are sent into space for many purposes.

Satellites can be any size—from a tiny package of instruments to a huge balloon. They can weigh a few pounds or many tons. They can be any shape—balls, hatboxes, tin cans, bell buoys, and cigar boxes.

Some satellites have orbits around the earth as near as 110 miles away. Some travel 22,300 miles from earth. A satellite's orbit is chosen by scientists in advance, according to the task the satellite must perform.

All satellites need electrical power to operate their equipment. The main source of this power is the sun. Satellites carry many solar cells on their outside surface. A solar cell is a device that uses sunlight to generate electricity; this electricity keeps the satellite's batteries charged.

Radio and television signals can be sent from one continent to another by means of communications satellites. Most communications satellites have receivers and transmitters. The receivers pick up radio and television broadcasts from a ground station.

Electronic devices then increase the strength of the broadcast signals. The transmitters send the broadcasts to a distant ground station, which may be on another continent.

An example of such a satellite is Telstar. Telstar I was launched by the United States in July, 1962. Direct television transmission between the United States and Europe was first made possible by Telstar I.

One type of communications satellite has a "stationary" orbit around the earth. It is at a distance of 22,300 miles above the earth and completes one orbit in 24 hours, the same time it takes the earth to rotate on its axis. Thus the satellite is always in the same place above the earth. The Early Bird satellite is this kind of satellite. Because its orbit is so high, it can transmit signals over very great distances.

WHAT ARE RADIO WAVES?

Did you know that the space around you is filled at all times with radio waves from nearby broadcasting stations? These waves cause minute vibrations in all the metal objects in the room. You cannot hear the vibrations until they become sound waves, and they become sound waves only when you turn on your radio.

A radio wave might be called a disturbance that moves out into space. When electrons move back and forth rapidly, we have a radio wave. Heat and light also travel through space in the form of waves. The difference is that radio waves have a much longer wavelength than either heat or light waves.

Radio waves travel through space in much the same way that waves travel when a pebble is dropped into water. The waves radiate in all directions from their source. Although all radio waves travel at a speed of about 186,000 miles a second, the number of radio waves that travel past a point in one second can vary greatly. This number is called the frequency.

One complete wavelength is called a cycle. So frequency is the number of complete cycles that take place in a second. If wavelength is short, the waves are close together; the crests are close together and follow each other quickly. If wavelength is long, crests are far apart and follow one another slowly. So long waves are of low frequency, because crests do not come as frequently as those of short waves.

High-frequency waves are measured in kilocycles, or thousands of cycles per second. On your radio, from left to right, are the numbers 540, 550, 560, and so on to 1600 kilocycles. Each number refers to a wave frequency. A radio program broadcasts its programs only on its own wave frequency.

The existence of radio waves was predicted long before they were actually discovered. The prediction was made in 1864 by James Maxwell. In 1888 a German physicist, Heinrich Hertz, demonstrated that the waves actually do exist, and travel through space.

WHAT IS A RADIO TELESCOPE?

When we look at stars and planets through a telescope, we see light waves that they send out. Light is a form of radiation. But stars send out other forms of radiation besides light.

Part of the radiation from stars is sent out as radio waves. Some of these waves can be detected by special radio receivers here on earth. The radio receivers collect and magnify the radio waves, just as ordinary telescopes collect and magnify the picture the light waves give. These radio receivers are called radio telescopes.

There are many kinds of radio telescopes, but all of them consist of two parts—an antenna and a radio receiver. The antenna is often a huge, spectacular-looking metal dish. It may be fitted on a movable stand or mounting, so that it can be pointed to any part of the sky.

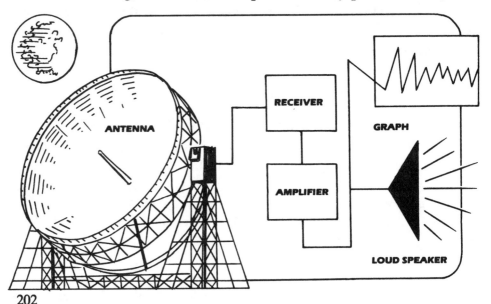

The large metal dish is what people usually think of when they think of a radio telescope. But the radio receiver is an equally important part. Without the receiver the huge antenna would be of no use.

Special kinds of radio receivers are needed to magnify, or amplify, the incoming waves. This is because the waves are often very weak. After the radio signals are amplified, they may be sent to a loudspeaker that lets the astronomer hear their hissing noise. Usually, however, a record of the radio waves is made on paper. The signals are written down in the form of a wavy line on a strip of paper.

Radio telescopes can operate in all kinds of weather, because radio waves are not affected by mist or fog or other kinds of bad weather. They can also be built in any place that is convenient, and don't have to be built on high ground or on mountains as optical telescopes must be.

Radio telescopes help astronomers learn facts about the universe that could not be learned in any other way we now have.

WHAT IS RADIO ASTRONOMY?

In 1931, a communications engineer working for Bell Laboratories was exploring radio frequency disturbances in the atmosphere that might interfere with a transoceanic telephone. He noticed that he was picking up a noise that didn't come from thunderstorms—but from somewhere in outer space! He discovered that he was able to pick up radiation from far away in our galaxy; and a new branch of astronomy was born—radio astronomy.

Radio astronomy works in two ways. By using special types of antennae, it picks up radiations sent out by objects in space. Some of these are "thermal" radiations, the radiations that any heated body emits in radio frequency waves. But there is also noise, or "cosmic static," which is picked up from outer space and is not thermal in origin.

Another way radio astronomy works is in sending signals out to such objects as meteors and the moon, and obtaining the reflection. This is the way radar works.

So far radio astronomy has been most useful in the study of meteors, the moon, the sun, and other planets. By bouncing back beams from meteors, we learn much about their orbits. By studying the moon with radio astronomy, we learn something about its surface. For example, even before men landed on the moon, radio astronomy led scientists to believe that its surface layers consisted of powdered rocks.

Perhaps the most exciting use of radio astronomy is about to begin—the search for messages from other worlds! A radio telescope has been developed that can detect a signal almost 50 trillion miles away. What kind of signal do scientists hope to pick up? They believe that if there is some civilization somewhere in outer space, and it wants to make its presence known, it would probably send out some very simple signal such as a series of numbers. It is also thought that the signals would be of the radio frequency of 1,420 megacycles, the frequency at which natural hydrogen emits radio energy in outer space.

INDEX